⊕RIGI

NEW WRITING F
BRITAIN'S OLDE⌄⌄ ⌄ ⌄⌄⌄⌄

C000176832

Risk-taking writing for risk-taking readers.

JM Originals was launched in 2015 to champion distinctive, experimental, genre-defying fiction and non-fiction. From memoirs and short stories to literary and speculative fiction, it is a place where readers can find something, well, *original*.

JM Originals is unlike any other list out there with its editors having sole say in the books that get published on the list. The buck stops with them and that is what makes things so exciting. They can publish from the heart, on a hunch, or because they just really, really like the words they've read.

Many Originals authors have gone on to win or be shortlisted for a whole host of prizes including the Booker Prize, the Desmond Elliott Award and the Women's Prize for Fiction. Others have been selected for promotions such as Indie Book of the Month. Our hope for our wonderful authors is that JM Originals will be the first step in their publishing journey and that they will continue writing books for John Murray well into the future.

Every JM Original is published with a limited-edition print run and bespoke cover designed by an up-and-coming illustrator from Liverpool John Moores University. This means every time you buy one of our covetable books, you're not only investing in an author's career but also building a library of (potentially!) valuable first editions. Writers need readers and we'd love for you to become part of our JM Originals community. Get in contact and tell us what you love about our books. We're waiting to hear from you.

JM ORIGINALS

Coming from JM Originals in 2023

She That Lay Silent-Like Upon Our Shore | **Brendan Casey**
A cunning fable about humanity's relationship with the natural world, crisis and religion from a daring new talent.

Stronger than Death | **Francesca Bratton**
A soaring, lyrical part-memoir, part-biography of modernist poet Hart Crane's final year in Mexico; the story of his mother's grief after his death; and the author's struggles with mental illness in the years she first discovered the power of Hart's poetry.

Stronger than Death

Hart Crane's Last Year in Mexico

Francesca Bratton

JM ORIGINALS

First published in Great Britain in 2023 by JM Originals
An imprint of John Murray (Publishers)

1

Copyright © Francesca Bratton 2023

A CIP catalogue record for this title is available from the British Library

Trade Paperback ISBN 9781529383379
ebook ISBN 9781529383386

Typeset in Minion Pro by Hewer Text UK Ltd, Edinburgh
Printed and bound in Great Britain by Clays Ltd, Elcograf S.p.A.

John Murray policy is to use papers that are natural, renewable and
recyclable products and made from wood grown in sustainable forests.
The logging and manufacturing processes are expected to conform
to the environmental regulations of the country of origin.

Carmelite House
50 Victoria Embankment
London EC4Y 0DZ

www.johnmurraypress.co.uk

John Murray Press, part of Hodder & Stoughton Limited
An Hachette UK company

For my own mother, Felicity

Contents

Contents

What the novelist does is to try to wipe the slate clean, and say, 'You don't know this man, but you're about to meet him.'

Hilary Mantel

Introduction

The Remorseless Line

April 1931. On the warmest day of the year so far, Hart Crane – advertising copyrighter, shipyard bolter-up, newspaper reporter, hod-carrier, munition-factory worker, bookseller, shipping clerk, alcoholic, poet – made his way to Pier Four on New York's East River to board the *Orizaba* to Mexico.

He had replaced his fraying clothes and paid off his debts. His advance from the Guggenheim Foundation was gone, along with a portion of his first quarter's allowance. In his suitcase he had a sailor outfit, a white pyjama suit and several pairs of dungarees – spoils from the previous day's shopping with the photographer Walker Evans. There had been a farewell gala party the night before. He had broken two months of sobriety and had a hangover.

Hart had stood by the harbour walls countless times, 'searching, thumbing the midnight on the piers', waiting for Emil's ship to come in, for a flash of his lover's blond hair against standard-issue navy: 'In all the argosy of your bright hair I dreamed / Nothing so flagless as this piracy', he wrote to Emil, 'Permit me voyage, love, into your hands . . .'

In his cabin, a fleck of paint on the harbour wall hovered up and down behind the glass of a small window as the ship moved slowly against the dock. Drinking again already, everything began to resemble something else. An apple was the sun's mimic, a distant friend's smile was replicated in the markings of the cabin's wooden walls, the music on the Victrola sounded like snow, like mechanical laughter.

It was just over a year since his masterpiece *The Bridge* was published, a long poem that vaults from the New York subway to the landscapes of his native Midwest and all between – what Hart called his 'grand synthesis of our America'. He planned to write a parallel epic, exploring pre-Columbian Mexican art, festivals and traditions.

But this hadn't always been the plan. His Guggenheim application, which he had dispatched to the Foundation the previous summer, described his intention to spend a year in France. The trip would, he told the selection committee, allow him to explore his interest in European literary traditions, 'classical and Romantic'. He wanted to contrast these strands of influence against 'emergent features of a distinctly American poetic conversation'.

Following news of the Foundation's award, and just a fortnight before Hart was due to sail, he travelled to Patterson, upstate New York, for the weekend with a dear friend, Malcolm Cowley, and his partner Muriel Maurer. Completely broke, and unable to find copywriting work in the wake of the Wall Street Crash, Hart had spent the previous summer camping in the area with a friend, before a cheap room became available with his regular landlady, Addie Turner. She threw him out after a fortnight, which seems to have been the average period of time Hart could be tolerated as a guest. He had left a number of his belongings in Patterson, and needed to collect his records, books, clothes and art objects before he sailed for France. Objects had an allure for Hart. He had various talismans, including a little duck that he hung from the window of his New York apartment at 110 Columbia Heights, where he started work on *The Bridge* in 1923.

The fields in Patterson were grey, frozen and patched with ice. Odd slashes of apricot would strike through the clouds in the morning, promising snow. On Sunday evening, having discovered his hosts' stash of alcohol (which his friends attempted to ration in his company), Hart became agitated. He was unable to focus on the through line of a conversation, shifting rapidly from long rhapsodic descriptions of his writing plans to his love of film and Marlene Dietrich. Her voice, he said, came straight from Tutankhamun's tomb. After dinner, he, Malcolm and Muriel made their way back to New York. Hart was silent in the touring car that drove them to the station and on the train ride home. He left Malcolm and Muriel at Grand Central Station with a warm but firm goodbye. Hart headed for the docks. This was the last time Malcolm would see his friend.

At some point over the weekend's boozy lunches and long walks a new idea had emerged. Piqued by Malcolm's stories of his travels in Mexico, and his discussions with another recently returned friend, the writer Waldo Frank, Hart decided to go to Mexico City. For an American tourist, the capital city would be relatively affordable. It offered the promise of realising a project he had long dreamt of, but for which he would find himself to be ill-equipped: a poetic drama centred around Montezuma and Cortés. On 27 March, Hart made his way to the New York office of the principal administrator of the John Simon Guggenheim Memorial Foundation, Henry Allen Moe. Hart explained his change of plans, and his idea to write a long poem exploring Mexican history and culture. Moe agreed, and assigned Hart to a group of Latin American Exchange Fellows.

Hart's plans sprang into motion, with firm warnings from both Moe and Frank to curb his drinking. When he was drunk, which was often, he was awful. He lost his sense of humour entirely. The warnings were, naturally, ineffectual. The day after Hart's meeting with Moe, Hart was thrown out of a party in the offices of the *New Republic* after trading punches with another guest. Hair mussed, he reappeared later in the evening, with the brass to request money for his cab. As he sobered up, his mood changed to remorse. He offered the quiet, embarrassed apologies of a polite child.

At noon the USS *Orizaba* sailed for Mexico. Hart's friends had joined him for a final drink and to wave him goodbye. The *Orizaba* boasted wicker lounges and velvet-clad bars. Its kitchens produced extravagant, fashionable meals. Wealthy passengers could eat Cuban lobster, mounds of iceberg lettuce topped with Roquefort dressing, Jell-O set in a Macedoine mould with whipped cream, preserved coconut and guava jelly.

Its captain, implausibly named Blackadder, was handsome, tanned and athletic. Hart made a note of the captain in his letters, declaring him 'very much a Dane', which I suspect was Hart's way of saying Blackadder was extremely attractive, like Hart's Danish sailor-lover Emil Opffer. A year later, in April

1932, Blackadder would write and send a telegram: 'Hart Crane went overboard at noon today. Body not recovered.' The short message was published in hundreds of syndicated newspapers that evening; this was how Grace Hart Crane would learn of her son's death, while on shift at the Carleton Hotel in Chicago where she was working as a hostess. The newspaper arrived before a barrage of telegrams all declaring the same news, the first from her former brother-in-law, Hart's uncle:

MESSAGE FORWARDED FROM CAPTAIN STEAM-SHIP ORIZABA UPON WHICH HART WAS RETURNING FROM MEXICO STATES HART FELL OVERBOARD WEDNESDAY NOON BODY NOT RECOVERED I GO TO NEW YORK TONIGHT FOR PARTICULARS WILL ADVISE YOU BESS JOINS SINCEREST SYMPATHY = N B MADDEN

In 2011, working on my doctoral research proposal, I came across William Logan's essay 'The Hart Crane Controversy'. After his review of a new edition of Hart Crane's poems prompted backlash in the pages of the *New York Times*, Logan wrote: 'Crane is one of the few who has votaries and devotees (Sylvia Plath is another). Whatever his flaws, personal or poetic, they pale before what some see as his genius. If you don't see the genius, all you have left are the flaws.'

Beyond this specious logic, the bulk of Logan's article deals with the contrasting accounts of Hart's death, ranging from the inconsequential to bizarre: did he fold his overcoat before he jumped? Was it a topcoat, or a jacket? Was he eaten by a shark? Did he wave?

To draw together Hart Crane and Sylvia Plath in this way is predictable, given both remarkable poets have found their work read back retrospectively, combed through by critics for premonitions of their deaths. This is a well-worn template, as these article titles make clear:

'Tortured Visionary: A Life of Hart Crane' (*Chicago Tribune*)
'How poets' words can foreshadow their suicides: John Berryman, Hart Crane and Sergei Esenin' (*Daily Telegraph*)
'Sylvia Plath: The Road to Suicide' (*Guardian*)
'Sylvia Plath's Suicide: Why Some Blamed Poetry' (*Time*)

For his friend, the writer Allen Tate, Hart's 'sensational death was morally appropriate', a fitting emblem for a life he judged to be disordered. 'I think it has some significance as a symbol of the "American" mind', wrote Tate.

Mental illness is not a muse, a version of the Romantic Aeolian harp, music made by the wind gently playing on the strings until they snap. I have only heard silence. Wasted hours piling up in a suffocating mass, the occasional moment of resistance. From the age of eighteen I existed in a state of detachment, as if experiencing the world through thick glass. This way of being was disrupted at regular intervals when violent flashbacks and hallucinations would break through the protective mechanism of dissociation.

Hart wrote frequently of the 'remorseless line' that separates reality and hallucination – a step away from what is real, a counterpoint. In 'Voyages', an ecstatic series of love poems to various sailors, including his long-term partner, Emil, Hart writes: 'but there is a line / You must not cross nor ever trust beyond it'. It has often been said that this refers to Hart's blackmail by an ex-lover – a reading I agree with – but I think he is getting at something beyond the horrors of that particular experience.

'Cutty Sark' features another sailor. The poem collages his mutterings, transcribing his scattered memories, his breaking into song, with these fragments tenuously linked by the poem's narrator. The poem is very much written from the other side of the crossed line, as distinctions between reality and hallucination dissolve into each other: 'I saw the frontiers gleaming of his mind', writes Hart, 'or are there frontiers – running sands sometimes / running sands – somewhere – sands running . . .'

I found Hart Crane at a time when my mind was collapsing in on itself, running, in the aftermath of a horrifying event. Imagine a cold beach: your daily task is to keep a vast pile of dry and bright white sand in the same shape. Night falls, the reaching belly of the horizon merges with the dark blue of the sky. You wake, you sleep, you wake: there is the sand. It was useful for me to think that these lines, gleaming frontiers, marked the territory of sanity. Once its contours have been exposed, there is no turning back.

After five years of increasing prescriptions and brief stints of extremely unhelpful therapy – at one the psychologist broke the ice by asking me to identify my first sexual urge – I was eventually diagnosed with post-traumatic stress disorder and assigned a specialist clinical psychologist. At the time of writing I have gone through this process twice: a slow decline, near total mental collapse, followed by intervention. I have told approximately fifteen medical professionals (strangers) the intimate details of my history during the process of these assessments. It is unusual to see these professionals more than once.

In our shed, just within the border of County Meath, sit two ring-binders filled with third-person narratives of a particular tangled thread of my life. I will not unspool it. I do not wish to testify here. In *Coriolanus*, in conversation with a fellow tribune, Junius Brutus remarks on the commander's refusal to share his battle injuries with his public – part patrician contempt, part refusal to have his experiences validated by the crowd:

> I heard him swear,
> Were he to stand for consul, never would he
> Appear i' the market-place nor on him put
> The napless vesture of humility,
> Nor showing, as the manner is, his wounds
> To the people, beg their stinking breaths.

Hart has had his wounds excavated in public, shown to the people by his interlocutors and critics, many of whom were his friends. Hart's departure for Mexico in 1931 on his Guggenheim Fellowship has been presented as a point of no return. This last year has been seen as marked by self-destructive creative drought, whereby Hart in his cups – the alcoholic *poète maudit* – is doomed to Baudelairean damnation in the Gulf of Mexico. It has accrued a morbid, exotic mythology, rooted in colonial narratives that associate Mexico with death. 'Mexico killed Hart', declared his friend and fellow Guggenheimer Lesley Byrd Simpson in one of the most crashingly stupid sentences written about the poet.

In newspaper obituaries after Hart's death and in the

recollections of his friends, Hart's mother, Grace, was an explanation or was to be looked at. She was glamorous, vain, hysterical, monstrous, frigid – cannibalistically possessive. An umbilical cord in the shape of a noose. Jocasta, weeping. She was difficult, certainly, judging by her letters and telegrams to her son. She would write desperately, explaining that he alone could rescue her and demanding his immediate presence: 'COME AT ONCE DESPERATELY ILL AT HOME ALONE ONLY YOU CAN HELP.'

I can't begin to assume Hart's state of mind on the day he stepped onto the USS *Orizaba*, en route to Mexico on 4 April 1931, or how it was making a brief return for his father's funeral that July, or how his long estrangement from his mother wore upon him. Nor can I guess how he felt stepping onto the same ship almost a year later, three days before he would jump from the railings, just hours after the boat had passed through Havana.

I do not think that his death was inevitable, teleological, coursing through his poetry, or that either of his parents can provide neat explanations for his psychological unease. I do not think that diagnosing Hart from a distance on the basis of letters, poems and the subjective reminiscences of friends is helpful or useful. I do not want to excavate his wounds, to attempt to find a narrative for his death. To state what should be obvious: I want to write about the man who was alive before he was dead.

Here I return to the poet from whom I sought comfort, and who I came to love by accident. At twenty, I was an undergraduate student in English at University College London. One afternoon between lectures, I was in a bookshop on Gower Street with my boyfriend. 'Here . . .' he said, passing the slim and purple book to me with his smoke-stubbed fingers, green eyes looking into green eyes. 'It's weird,' he said, 'you'll love it.' I took the book home and read it obsessively. I tried to puzzle out Hart's poems in my perversely structured and digressive undergraduate essays, always littered with typographical errors and written at odd hours, in between classes and shifts in the stinking bar where I worked.

This book aims to capture Hart's vitality, his blurring of what was and what was not real. I have found great solace in the fragmented, dissolving and reforming minds that populate Hart's poems. His poems teach the value of being unsure, with truths, half-truths and disguised details of his life woven through them. He had, as he wrote, a 'dense metaphorical habit', juxtaposing and layering images – he called this, somewhat ironically, 'the logic of metaphor'. He was 'more interested in the so-called illogical impingements of the connotations of words on the consciousness' than he was keen to preserve 'their logically rigid significations'.

In one of my favourite examples, he refers to the suspension structure of the Brooklyn Bridge as 'choiring strings', getting at both its harp-like cable structure and the sounds that he could hear as he walked across it. Hart's poetry teaches a radical way of reading, one that is uncertain and vulnerable. His poems resist the closure of paraphrase: we cannot gloss 'choiring strings' as 'suspension wires' because it does not capture the sound. Instead we have to talk around it, adding suggested details, such as the sound of the wind. Perhaps we can add more: that he walked across the bridge at night with his great love, Emil, and they could see the outline of the bridge from their bedroom in Brooklyn. His poems invite radically open, mutable interpretation. They privilege not quite knowing.

In this book I pull at the threads found in three lives: Hart's, Grace's and my own. Biography is the conjuring of ghosts, an attempt to offer a glimpse of something or someone absent. Autobiography is perhaps the same project, necessitating the construction of numerous past selves, but the materials and fragments are wrenched from within, rather than gathered piecemeal from archives, interviews, endless books, newspapers, weather reports. As Carmen Maria Machado writes, 'The memoir, at its core, is an act of resurrection.' Both memoir and biography cast one version of the subject, determined by the book's writer. There are endless others.

In Hart's portions of the book, I make nothing up. Rizal Gaultier, an acquaintance of Hart's, wrote to their mutual friend Sam Loveman, after Hart's death:

> Although he and I were not friends, I came to know, through you and through what I saw, many intimate details of his life. If ever his biography is written they will be ignored; and to a disadvantage, for there is no doubt those 'intimate details' reveal the man Crane as he was. I intend keeping all the newspaper clippings that I can get hold of.

I follow the intimate traces in the writing and photographs he left behind, but I do not invent between the gaps in his archive and his letters, imagining the erotic detail of his relationships. There is a moral imperative to preserve historical reality as best we can. There are facts, and history is what is written around them. I preserve the violence that exists in omissions, the gaps in Hart's archives: the letters his mother burned, the disavowals, the beatings he withstood when he eyed the wrong man on the pier or the deck of a ship.

Grace, Hart's mother, like most women, does not have the luxury of an archive. Her letters to her son are preserved, as is the gown she wore on the night she married his father, while newspaper reports reveal the scandal of her second divorce. Other than official records and these evocative but slight documents, preserved due to her son's fame, there is nothing. In Grace's sections, therefore, I take liberties, imagining a life between absences in the historical record. They are based on facts, but contain inventions.

The final resurrection is that of my own past self, as my voice weaves in between mother and son. The story of my love of Hart's poetry emerges against the backdrop of my struggles with mental illness and the loss of my relationship with my father. I try to capture an intimacy often excluded from standard biographies and literary criticism, which prizes objectivity and the concealment of one's emotional response to a work. This central conceit requires cloaking the fact that each writer we discuss or write about at length is our own version of that writer. There are as many Harts as there are readers.

Here I find myself stepping into that stream of Hart's mad 'votaries and devotees'. I still use the same copy of Hart Crane's *Complete Poems* that I bought in 2009, layered with notes, midnight-blue spine sealed with cheap brown tape. I discarded (thankfully) a copy of *The Bridge* that I typed and printed out for finals, tourniqueted with lines that marked allusions and long-reaching rhymes. Rhyme is enchanting. Rhyme forges ideas between things through the sheer accident of sound. The unconnected becomes connected, sometimes dangling for dozens of lines before their reunion with the principal sound. These annotations were my attempt to make the fugitive shape of *The Bridge* cohere. I returned to this bizarre method at Oxford close to the brink of mental collapse: writing on T. S. Eliot's *Four Quartets*, I spread a similar collection of hand-typed sheets over my college room. I secretly thought I was a genius. I secretly thought I was a moron. I can remember the colours but not the code ascribed to the lines that dragged, incised and quartered the poems.

This surgical approach continued through my doctoral research, which was bibliographically inclined, years dedicated to finding and collating 'Crane's' publications in literary journals. Piece by piece I tried to reconstruct his career, mapping out the development of his poetry, his relationships with editors, writers, publishers – a biography that was not a biography: the story of the poet written at a deliberate remove from the cartoonish sketches that pervade discussions of his life.

The same year I first came across Hart Crane's poetry, a student ran out of our seminar on Sylvia Plath. I was both embarrassed and envious of her performance. I was intensely secretive about my suffering, and couldn't imagine making it visible – even if indirectly, through a response to a poet. The energy of my own immediate responses to poetry were gradually transmuted into codes, spreadsheets and meticulously collected bibliographic data, metrical analyses, endless marginalia. Now I see that through his complex use of language, close-knit metaphors and layered images, Hart taught me the value of ambiguity and of not quite knowing – call it caveats or call it, as Keats did, negative capability. Years ago now, the book pristine in my hands for the first time, and leaning into the shop's black bookshelves, I opened the collection at random points, stumbling upon 'Voyages':

> But now
> Draw in your head, alone and too tall here.
> Your eyes already in the slant of drifting foam;
> Your breath sealed by the ghosts I do not know:
> Draw in your head and sleep the long way home.

And so I did.

Party on the Orizaba

Hart's five-day journey from New York to Veracruz was at turns dull and surreal. He drank heavily and was observed by other passengers swaying along the decks, smiling with a beer in one hand and a glass in the other, cigar balanced at the corner of his mouth.

On 7 April, the *Orizaba* made her way past the Morro Castle guarding Havana harbour and over the last remains of the USS *Maine*, mysteriously sunk in 1898 (the catalyst of the Spanish–American War), before docking in Havana. At about 5 p.m., Hart disembarked the ship to eat dinner with two new friends, both doctors and research scientists, Hans Zinsser and Maximiliano Ruiz Castañeda. En route, he dashed off a quick note to his friend Lorna Dietz, a translator: 'There are magnificent people and things ahead. How valid it all turns out to be!'

Hart had first met Zinsser at a gala party the night before the *Orizaba* sailed, introduced by a mutual friend. Slim, with angular, sharp features and deep-set eyes, Zinsser was a

Harvard bacteriologist and sometime poet. He had spent his career engaged in work on Brill–Zinsser disease, a variant of typhus that can remain in the body, latent, for many years before reactivation – forming new epicentres of infection.

Castañeda was working as Zinsser's assistant on a research project to develop a safe typhus vaccine. The two doctors had smuggled dozens of infected rats onto the *Orizaba* to compare strains of the disease found in Mexico City and New York. The rats were caged and hidden in Castañeda's rooms. The two doctors and Hart spent the journey drinking beer and high-balls, discussing poetry and the typhus project. Hart would retreat to Castañeda's room, Zinsser wrote later, where he would sit and stare at the rats. The rats unknowingly crossed almost one and a half thousand nautical miles of ocean – no doubt continuing with their activities, if slowing as the disease took hold: worrying at each other's fur, their yellow teeth probing and scratching, pulling insistently at the fibres of the fabric covering the cage, drawing the material through the bars.

That evening, Hart, Zinsser and Castañeda made their way to the Diane cafe. In Havana, modern buildings were laid out in neoclassical and art-nouveau styles, set against the ornate baroque of the colonial architecture. In the old quarters of the city, trams whirred through the busy streets, pursued by cars. On foot, people pressed against each other as they passed on the pavement, in streamlined dresses, shirtsleeves, suits, the occasional straw hat. Shopfronts were thrown open, women sat in lines having their nails polished in the heat, the lacquer drying quickly in neat, gently pointed ovals.

Tables were set outside, laid with checked cloths and carafes and glasses waiting for wine. At the Diane, the two doctors watched Hart drink two bottles of Chablis while writing postcards, then loaned the poet money for two quarts of Bacardi. Hart recorded a version of their conversation in his poem 'Havana Rose'. He put words in the doctor's mouth, offering guidance:

> "You cannot heed the negative –, so might go on
> to undeserved doom . . . must therefore loose yourself
> within a pattern's mastery that you can conceive, that
> you can yield to – by which also you
> win and gain that mastery and happiness which
> is your own from birth."

Both poet and doctor were travelling in pursuit of their great masters, collecting impressions and ideas that might be assimilated in service of a larger, mythic project. Hart did not finish his Mexican epic, nor did Zinsser manage to create an effective vaccine. But in 1935, *Rats, Lice and History*, Zinsser's biography of typhus, was laid out on bookstalls. The book tells the heroic story of the microorganism's struggle for survival, and features a brief comment on Hart, 'a man of great talent, appealing and tragic, for he was very sick in spirit'. The poet and the doctor were both pursuing patterns – grand, overarching narrative shapes. One artistic, chasing ideas and rhythms through language, the other an ancient disease that, through mutations, ensured its survival. The three talked and drank. At 9.30 p.m. they returned to the ship, and Hart disappeared to his cabin with the rum.

It was a few hours later. Dozens of teeth glinted yellow in the waves. The teeth rose slightly in the dark swell, then lurched downwards and away from the ship. A crate housing a group of typhus-infected grey rats thrown from the deck of the *Orizaba*

17

had opened on impact. Gagging on saltwater, the rodents swam towards Havana, streaked by moonlight. They moved swiftly, with an athleticism that belied their rounded shape.

The cold water had revived the rodents. Zinsser and Castañeda had found them sprawled in their cage, barely breathing, and decided to throw them overboard. The ship was still docked, freight shifting on and off the wharf. The doctors waited anxiously as the rats briefly seemed to paw at the half-submerged rope of another boat. Eventually they lost their struggle against the current and disappeared.

Hart appeared, staring into the black and grey swell. Zinsser recalled how Hart seemed to see the rats long after they had drowned. He supposed that Hart was reminded of a disturbing incident during his six-day imprisonment at La Santé, Paris, in 1929 – the prison that had famously housed Apollinaire, for supposedly aiding and abetting the theft of the *Mona Lisa* and a number of Egyptian statuettes. Hart had been jailed for fighting with waiters at the Café Sélect (waiters were to be his perennial antagonists once again in Mexico City). That night, Hart had seen a Parisian rat as large and hairy as a poodle parading around his cell.

It might have been the DTs: delirium tremens brought on by alcohol withdrawal, a swift descent into confusion, with shaking, an irregular heart rate, sweating, hallucinations. But watching the waves from the *Orizaba*, Hart seems to have been firmly planted on the other side of the 'remorseless line' – the sands running as his perception of his surroundings warped. At times I too have lost my grip on what was and what was not real. I have regularly smelt and tasted foul things that weren't there: my boyfriend grew used to tasting my food, so convinced was I that a saucepan or glass had been spiked with urine.

During finals I hallucinated a man attempting to break into my shared flat in Kentish Town. I crawled into the kitchen on my stomach, snaked my arm up onto the counter, grasped a knife. I grabbed an empty terracotta flowerpot as I made my way back into my room, hiding behind the high-backed sofas I had arranged like a cat bed in its centre. I heard the clack of the gate at the bottom of the outdoor stairs: my flatmate, Hannah. At that sound, and Hannah's call from the hallway, I realised the intruder wasn't real. I looked down, taking in the hastily arranged weapons in my lap.

Stood next to the doctors at the rail of the ship, still hallu-cinating, Hart began to speak. His voice was deep and loud – too loud for comfort: sailors were shifting freight off the ship, and Zinsser was agitated that their illicit jettison of cargo would be discovered. Circling the image, lines that would become 'Havana Rose' came to Hart – the beginning of a new poem:

> The Doctor has thrown rats into the harbor of Havana.
> The Doctor has thrown typhus rats into the water.
> There will be typhus in Havana.
> The Doctor has thrown rats into the harbor.

Hart could not be moved from the railings. Hearing foot-steps on the decking, Zinsser and Castañeda ducked behind a lifeboat. The first officer, Jensen, appeared. Hart, obviously drunk and muttering, his brown eyes dancing between Jensen, the waves and the rats, recounted the story, pointing at the rodents climbing the sides of the boats – they had long drowned, but he could still see them, their water-slicked coats gleaming. The Cuban port officer appeared. Zinsser and

Castañeda slid across the deck, escaping along the gangway to wait in Zinsser's cabin.

Zinsser heard a loud clatter, and Hart shouting: 'I am telling the truth! There are rats all over the harbour, and the rats have typhus.' There was a slam. Hart had been shut in his cabin for the remainder of the night.

The following morning, Blackadder strode the decks, looking for the passenger who had caused the previous night's disruptions. The poet, beer in hand once again, ran directly into the captain's broad chest. Hart, luckily, had momentarily forgotten the rats, and the two had a brief conversation. Hart was charming, as he could be.

On 9 April the ship docked at Veracruz. Zinsser bribed the port authorities, and he and Castañeda smuggled their cargo off the ship. The next day, Hart and the two doctors took the train to Mexico City, rats in tow.

Zinsser offers me a tempting image. In his autobiography he writes that soon after hearing of Hart's death, Castañeda made the same journey on the *Orizaba* with his wife. Timing their journey from Havana carefully, they scattered petals at the approximate spot where Hart jumped. I imagine the couple buying armfuls of flowers in Havana, large bouquets from a street vendor. I picture an elderly woman, as in photographs of the period, sipping coffee in the centre of a vast stall of densely packed blooms in every colour, pots perched on stools of increasing height. At noon the following day, perhaps they threw armfuls of orange lilies, white peonies and pink roses into the water. Yes, they were caught by the wind as they fell, scattering a distance from the boat. 'Rose leaves, when the rose is dead, / Are heap'd for the beloved's bed', wrote Shelley, also lost to water. So perfect, how the hundreds of petals swirled in the water, as the waves crest and crest in the propeller's wake, breathing orange, pink and purple garlands into the air, as the sheen of colour faded as the ship drew away.

2

'Why do you not come to me alone?'

A formal dinner: I sat next to an eminent scholar of modernist poetry. It was 2011, just two months since my graduation from University College London, and early in the first term of my master's. I drank the wine far too quickly, battling against the strange quilted wings of my gown, which repeatedly flung themselves onto the table. At some point the scholar asked which poets I was interested in. 'Hart Crane,' I replied. Seeing his face, I hastily added '. . . and Marianne Moore.' 'She is the more interesting poet,' he said firmly. 'He attracts dilettantes. Crane scholars have a particular reputation.'

I extracted an escaped wing from my glass and tucked it over my shoulder. Dancing before piles of green beans, boiled potatoes and an embarrassing stuffed courgette laid across my plate, the contemporary poets were cartoonishly resurrected by the professor. Hart, the alcoholic, over-sexed, violent, uncontrollable, over-reaching high school dropout, incapable of realising his ambitions (culminating, of course, in his death), versus Moore, the Presbyterian emblem of restraint, likely virgin, Bryn Mawr-educated genius editor, collector of fragments, tricorn hat-wearing baseball fan. Admirers of Hart's poetry were unfailingly mad, esoteric, obsessive and, I infer, perhaps queer. All to be avoided, it would seem.

In November 1927, Hart moved to Altadena, just to the north of LA. At first, the world seemed to open up out west: Hart found queer Hollywood, with parties and film-star lovers. But the shine quickly wore off. Hart stayed just seven months, but in that short time his beloved maternal grandmother died, his mother suffered a psychological breakdown and Hart's relationship with Grace disintegrated, and he was subjected to a terrifying attack while out with Emil near the San Pedro dock. His drinking grew significantly worse, his alcoholism appearing to enter a new stage. Significant gaps appear in Hart's story during these months, thanks to Grace's destruction of letters that mentioned their arguments.

Hart had quit his job as a bookseller in a shop on 57th Street, New York, and moved to California to work as an assistant to a wealthy young stockbroker, Herbert Wise. He moved into Wise's house at 2160 Mar Vista Avenue, Altadena and was employed as a companion of sorts, but their relationship was platonic. He explained the dynamic to his old friend and confidant William Wright, reassuring him that 'when I become a concubine you shall be told all the dirt'. For free lodgings and a stipend, he was employed to discuss literature with 'Herb', and regale him with stories of his adventures out on the tear in LA. In theory, Wise was working on a novel, but Hart never saw him write. He seemed to want to play at a literary lifestyle, with Hart as his main prop – the roaring boy kept as a pet for his entertainment.

At first, Hart revelled in the comfort of his new surroundings, the absurdity of Wise's three cooks (one of whom was Viennese), a luxurious shower and expensive port every evening. 'What will I do when faced again with Mrs Turner's cold turnips I don't know!' he joked. Hart had met Wise through Eleanor Fitzgerald, the business manager of Greenwich Village's famous experimental theatre, the Provincetown Playhouse (its players had included Djuna Barnes, Eugene O'Neill and E. E. Cummings). Wise, 'a millionaire neurotic' according to Hart, wanted 'a secretary who can talk to him about Eliot, Spengler, metaphysics, and what not.' The banker saw Hart as the perfect companion for his raucous parties in his grand house, fuelled by bootlegged liquor.

Wise's circle offered Hart a gateway into the world of queer Hollywood. The parties often lasted days: 'all flesh', Hart wrote . . . 'And wine and music and such nights – WHOOPS!!!!!!!' Many years later, the writer Nathan Asch recounted one of Hart's anecdotes, in which Hart found himself in the bath with a strangely beautiful but 'worn looking' man. It was, Hart claimed, only after the actor had insisted on going down on Hart that he realised he was a famous, ageing film star.

Hart's drinking quickly landed him in jail. His description of the arrest, within a fortnight of his arrival, reveals the twin lives he led: a more open existence with Wise and his circle, and another, forced into concealment. Hart was playing with somebody's lost Airedale terrier in the street at 3 a.m. An officer approached. The officer asked Hart what he was doing. Hart shouted back: 'Why the hell do you want to know?!!!' He was arrested and hauled into a police van. En route to the Clark Street Station where he would be locked up for the night, he went through his pockets, emptying out the window any incriminating traces of lovers, 'billets doux, dangerous addresses'.

Wise's house provided Hart with a haven (or a 'ménage' as he called it), at least as far as his romantic life was concerned, but he found the arrangement claustrophobic. The house was all 'bad furniture and bathrooms', Hart complained. He was preoccupied with the noise of the house and neighbourhood: fountains poured and mockingbirds sang their glissades unrelentingly in the garden, their music undercut by dogs barking. The people of Altadena talked louder. Actors 'blazed'. Charlie Chaplin seemed 'disappointing' in the California light when Hart happened upon him in a restaurant. He was less radiant, less handsome than their first meeting in 1923, which had lasted an evening, night and a morning. On the radio, the evangelist preacher Aimee McPherson shouted her sermons from the Angelus Temple in Los Angeles. Attendees were carried out, seized with spiritual convulsions, their passage flanked by palm trees, fronds shuffling in the wind like brushes on a drum. Even the geraniums were abrasive. They shook all night, Hart said, disturbing his sleep. Writing was nearly impossible.

Eventually Hart grew bored. 'I have already limousined around enough,' he complained. He felt that the excesses of LA – expensive parties, large houses, extravagant meals – masked the 'aridity of the social life here'. Hollywood in the new 'age of celluloid' was a 'Pollyanna greasepaint pinkpoodle paradise', wrote Hart. Its films were binges of 'everlasting stereotyped sunlight'. Directors, actors, writers were 'sylphlike robots' constructing films out of 'millions of mechanical accessories'.

At Christmas he took a trip to Santa Monica, staying at the Breaker Club. He spent his days walking along the beach, listening to the gulls and watching the pelicans, who eyed him over their long, coral beaks before lifting their legs and hauling themselves up, wings curving inwards, grasping at the air.

As Wise's assistant, Hart's duties were vague. Wise seemed to want Hart as a kind of drunk fool, living vicariously through his employee's stories. This was despite the obvious, worsening physical signs of Hart's illness: his face was red and puffy with the drink. His hair was turning from silver to white. For Hart, with alcoholism and his reliance on his circle of trusted friends, the job was disastrous. By March, he had had enough of his undefined role, the superficial meetings with countless numbers of his employer's friends, and Wise's interminable amateur 'psychoanalysis of every book, person, sausage and blossom'. Hart quit as soon as Wise found a boyfriend. He turned his attention to finding a job in the film industry as a scriptwriter and finishing *The Bridge* – though he was aggravated by his mother's insistence that he try acting. Probably overwritten or destroyed, there was once a reel of Hart and his benefactor Otto Kahn, an investment banker and patron of the arts, talking outside the Los Angeles Ambassador Hotel. 'At least I have "broken in" the movies in one way,' he told Cowley.

Hart's move to California was partly motivated by his mother. In October 1927, she had rented a cottage in Hollywood with her mother, Elizabeth Hart, and urged her son to join them. The job with Wise provided an opportunity for Hart to live nearby, but I wonder if the relative openness of life with Wise in Altadena created a sharp contrast with the closeted existence he was forced into when visiting his mother and grandmother. He went twice a week, observing their constant arguments with Elizabeth's live-in nurse.

For Grace and Elizabeth, LA was a relief at first. Elizabeth was kind with a wry smile, and she adored her grandson. By 1927, she had spent fourteen years without her husband, Clinton Orestes Hart, who died in 1913. She baked excellent cherry pies. She and her husband had been wealthy, keeping servants and a cook. Elizabeth was a Christian Scientist, persuaded into the faith by Grace shortly after Grace had moved back into the Harts' large home on 1709 East 115th Street, Cleveland, in 1908. Grace and Clarence Arthur Crane (known as C.A.), Hart's father and Grace's first husband, had been separated for a time. After C.A. left, Grace had suffered a psychological collapse and was admitted into a sanatorium. Grace, in intense psychological pain, found comfort in the Christian Scientists' belief that the mind could be trained to transcend any kind of earthly suffering. Even C.A., desperate to secure the affections of his estranged wife, briefly flirted with Mary Baker Eddy's teachings, though he had been raised as a Methodist. Hart dabbled and was sent to a Christian Scientist Sunday school. Later he said that he affected interest in the religion, trying to please his mother.

Elizabeth liked to tell stories. An old friend of Hart's from Cleveland, the bookseller and poet Sam Loveman, recalled how Elizabeth would tell them stories from the previous century. It seemed impossible – more than a lifetime ago – but, as a young bride, Elizabeth and her new husband had caught a glimpse of Lincoln's funeral train as it passed through Cleveland after his assassination in 1865. They rode into the city together on 28 April. It was raining hard. A line of white horses stood in the public square, harnessed to a pagoda-lidded catafalque. The horses waited, their gazes directed forward with blinkers, as the crowd – including Elizabeth and Clinton – snaked by.

The weather in California soothed Elizabeth. It was warm, even as the autumn turned, and the garden remained full of colour in winter. Grace was emerging from her second divorce. Grace had been desperate to leave a city containing, now, two ex-husbands. On 19 April 1927, a Tuesday, Grace had appeared before the court in Cleveland to finalise her divorce from Charles Curtis, an insurance adjuster seventeen years her senior. She had tried to make things work with Charles, insisting he and Hart wrote to each other. 'Nothing would make me happier than your marriage', her son had told her. But don't 'marry a mere moneybag', he urged her, 'it has always hurt me to hear you jest about such matters.' Grace was terrified, 'Yes I think I am in love or something, & I do not want to be – it is slavery . . . I just feel myself slipping, slipping, slipping.' Hart had met Charles briefly in September 1924, finding him unremarkable.

During the divorce proceedings, Grace was ridiculed in the press – the root of her frequent characterisation as greedy, hypochondriac, ridiculous. 'Denied Car, She Seeks Divorce: Wife of Wade Park Manor Insurance Adjustor Holds $250 insufficient', wrote the *Cleveland News*. 'Says Mate, 67, Let Love Cool', was the *Cleveland Press*'s line. Grace sued for alimony; Charles petitioned for divorce on the grounds of 'neglect and extreme cruelty'. So ended their year-long marriage, just under a decade after Grace's divorce from C.A., who ran a successful confectionery business.

Grace became very unwell in the aftermath of her second divorce. It was part of a pattern, mirroring the breakdowns she suffered after her separation from C.A. in 1908 and 1917, when the couple divorced. In the spring of 1927, Grace's psychological health had declined rapidly, and she had been admitted to hospital in Cleveland for two weeks. Once again, she relied on Hart's emotional support while he withdrew, leaving letters unanswered. She even wrote to Otto Kahn, seeking money and Hart's whereabouts. Eventually Hart did visit, Ohio drawing him away from writing trips to Patterson, Martinique and the Isle of Pines. To not see her would be a 'betrayal', she told him in a surviving letter. Surveying the detritus of her life, Grace decided to move to California, taking her mother with her.

Meanwhile, Hart's stepmother, Frances Kelly Crane, had died that same January. Frances and C.A. had been married for just under ten years. Hart had not heard from his father between November 1926 and March 1927, when he wrote with news of Frances's death. After C.A. emerged from his silence, grief seems to have enabled father and son to begin to erode the emotional distance between them. In the spring of 1927 C.A. frequently came to New York to see his son, who would travel down from Patterson, where he was spending time at Addie Turner's. Hart's presence soothed his grieving father. 'I would have done well to keep you in New York another day, for I seem to be no good when I am left alone,' C.A. told his son. Hart had other reasons to visit the city: his new lover, a sailor known only as Phoebus Apollo in letters to his trusted friend Wilbur Underwood, who had been a poet in his youth. Phoebus – bright Apollo, protector – was a refuge from Hart's family troubles.

At some point during his stay, Hart invited Grace to Altadena. According to Grace's recollections, on the first night of her trip Hart discussed his homosexuality with his mother for the first time. What we know of Grace's reaction can only be glimpsed at through her interview with Hart's first biographer, Philip Horton, the account filtered through memory, and shaped by the writer, who describes Hart's confession of his 'aberration'. Horton writes that Grace reacted neutrally, but adds that she decided to spend the night at a hotel, removing herself from her son. Hart interpreted her decision to stay elsewhere as an indictment of his sexuality, but continued to visit and write to Grace.

Hart knew that 'life isn't easy anywhere', and Grace and Elizabeth's problems soon showed themselves. Though she was still lively, Elizabeth's health was failing and the two were gradually forced to sell off their stocks and bonds to pay for her health care. Grace's psychological health began to break down once again as Elizabeth grew increasingly unwell. Grace found it hard to care for her mother. She found it hard to rouse herself out of bed. On 20 March, Hart moved out of Wise's 'ménage' and into Grace and Elizabeth's cottage to help care for his grandmother.

Four days later he made a doomed, forty-mile trip out to San Pedro to visit Emil. Emil's ship, the *California*, was due to arrive in San Pedro on the 24th. The two exchanged letters and made plans to meet on the docks. The evening ended with the pair brutally beaten. Accompanied by a young French sailor, Hart and Emil had got spectacularly drunk at a nearby speakeasy. At some point that night, after 'many bottles of dubious gin and whisky' the three were propositioned by another group of men. The newcomers suggested they took a hotel room together to 'finish their fire water' (or, at least, this was the code Hart used in letters). Instead, the three were jumped in the street, with Emil nearly 'spirited away' by the gang. Emil was virtually unconscious. Somehow, Hart and the French sailor dragged Emil back to his bunk on the *California*, where he lay 'as though he were nearing the pearly gates'. Hart's watch was stolen, as well as the minimal cash he had on him. Emil had won $100 in a craps game the previous night – gone. Emil was headed up to San Francisco. Hart hoped he might catch 'E' again on his journey home.

Hart's letters about the incident to his friends are euphemistic and full of silences. He was unable to fully explain what had happened. It seems clear that it had been a trap, a homophobic attack. Hart was terrified that Emil wouldn't want to see him again, perhaps fearing that his rambunctious behaviour had drawn unwelcome attention their way – plus he had been 'more emphatic' in his wishes to move to the hotel room. 'Life is nothing if not exciting whenever Emil happens to land', wrote Hart instead, adding that Emil 'always seems to get the hardest end of things'. He had experienced this type of violence before. It would happen again.

Living together again, Grace was shocked by Hart's drinking and, I suspect, frustrated by her son's partial explanations for his bruises and unease. 'The Cranes never knew the struggle I have had with it', she explained to Sam Loveman in a letter shortly after Hart's death. In May, Elizabeth died. Grace took to her bed entirely. Hart wrote that during this period, 'excessively hysterical conditions arose between me and my family' as mother and son prepared for and then sat with grief.

It has been said by Hart's biographers, without compelling evidence, that Grace grew jealous, madly so, of Hart's other relationships – even of the time he spent with lovers. It is said that she pressured him to become an actor, fulfilling her own youthful ambitions. What is certain is that Hart felt that he had fallen into a fugue state, exhausted by his mother's shifting

31

moods. He interpreted these as manipulations, confident, he wrote, that 'she had completely subdued me to a kind of idiotic jelly of sympathetic responses.' 'I carried it through', he explained, 'packing by infinitesimal degrees and labyrinthine subterfuges . . . until on the appointed hour the taxi drove up with darkened lights – and I was on my way'. Hart left for New York. Grace would never see her son again.

Hart was still two years away from finishing *The Bridge*. He had difficulty tying together the complex strands of the poem in its final stages. One particularly troublesome section was 'Indiana'. The poem ends with a mother calling out to her son: 'Come back to Indiana – not too late!', 'oh, I shall always wait'. At the time that he wrote these lines, and for what remained of his life, Hart and Grace were estranged. From late May 1928 he did not return any of Grace's letters.

At the time of Hart's death, Grace was working at the Carleton Hotel in Oak Park in Chicago. She had been in the job for two years. In her letters to Sam, she was coy about her job description: she described herself variously as a hostess and manager, but the work appeared to be back-breaking as she cleaned, dusted and waited on guests. In the years since Hart's departure, Grace had been forced to sell her belongings. The crash had destroyed her finances. As she told Sam, she sold her diamonds 'for a song' and, for the first time in her life, worked in a series of service jobs, moving from California to Illinois, New York City, and New Jersey before her own death in 1947.

She discovered the news in the paper. After Hart's death, Grace inherited her son's correspondence. Among other batches, she destroyed all letters from the period that mentioned their relationship, including those between Hart and his friends. She also burned intimate letters, destroying the records of Hart's relationships (there are letters attributed to be by Emil in the archive, but these are believed to be fakes). Grace was particularly angry about a Bob from Tuscaloosa (another sailor), who she judged to be an 'infantile creature', based on his sexually explicit letters.

At the same time, Grace was desperate to piece together the last years of Hart's life. And she did 'always wait', always did continue to call to Hart – even after his death. As a Christian Scientist, for Grace there was no sin, disease, or death. The material world is an illusion. In 2013 in Hart's archive at Columbia University, I found a transcript of Grace's attempts to contact her son through a series of seances, stretching across a number of years. I was caught off guard by the document, reading through it quickly, and pushing it back into the file. Unusually, I did not photograph it – as I did each potentially useful fragment – but I do remember describing it to my doctoral supervisor.

Some years later, I recalled finding the crumbling butter-coloured pages – my fingers gently lifting a new page, electric-blue plastic ovals guarding my nails from my teeth. But I didn't quite trust the memory, having recently emerged from a period of decline followed by psychiatric intervention. I sent the archivists a baffling email. I emphasised the 'strangeness' of the document, simultaneously noting that I had seen it, and querying its existence. I added pointlessly that: 'I was intrigued by this at the time as a document of her grief/ perhaps evidence of her own thwarted creativity, but did not get scans.'

Rereading the email now, I realise that the defensive tone was borne from a fear that I had imagined the transcript. During that period of research, based at the Library of Congress, but dashing between archives and repositories along the East Coast, I dreamed vividly of libraries, imagining new magazines and other oddities. In a tiny, white-barred room at Thompson-Markward Hall, a Christian Home established in 1833 to help young women take up positions on Capitol Hill (no men past the lobby: it is known locally as 'the nunnery'), I dreamed of the archives in my sleep.

My fear that the transcript was the product of my imagination was not without cause. I wrote the email with prior embarrassments in mind, where my delusions had collided with reality. In the first months of 2011, I had been convinced that the Chief Rabbi would be performing Prince William and Kate Middleton's marriage ceremony in Westminster Abbey. This was thanks to a waking dream, a hallucination, where I conjured a full edition of BBC Radio 4's *Today* programme. The ceremony was to be a celebration of multi-faith Britain, the presenters announced: a startling change of course for the Royal Family with enormous implications for the monarch as head of the Church of England. On the day of the wedding, I walked into the kitchen to make coffee, blithely commenting on this interesting fact to Hannah, who was cooking an extravagant breakfast. We cackled over it as I made the coffee, emptying an old, abandoned filter and shaking fresh grounds into the pot.

A few days after I had contacted the archivist, a scan appeared in my email inbox, a long transcription of Grace's seances with a medium, Frances, in New York City in the early 1940s. The transcript begins half way through, covering just under a year of meetings. The first record is dated 18 August

1940, but the group had met several times before, judging by the caveat typed at the top of the page: '(After waiting an unusually long time for contact)'. The final record is dated 9 July 1941. Scrolling through the document, my relief was twofold: the transcript was real and, though patchy and full of gaps, it was incredible. Reading through it, I felt ashamed for discarding it when searching through the archive for further evidence of her famous son's genius.

It appeared that a circle of women had gathered for these meetings. The documents record Frances's presence, of course, as well as Grace's dear friends Kathryn Edwards and Kathryn Kenney, who visited from Cleveland. It is possible that Sam was occasionally present at these evenings. At the very least, Grace passed him messages, with several communications (including poems) received during the meetings dedicated: 'To Sam Loveman'. Sam and Grace first met in Cleveland in 1918 when Hart was still a teenager. Sam had known Grace's son and her mother, both gone. Grace chased Hart through letters to Sam after he left LA. She wrote again after Hart died, trying to make sense of what had happened. A close friendship developed through correspondence, until Grace moved to New York in October 1933.

'I hope you will credit him with having a mother,' Grace told Waldo Frank, the writer friend of Hart's who inspired him to go to Mexico, and whom Grace commissioned to edit Hart's *Collected Poems*. In fact, it was Grace who gave Hart his poet's name. Born Harold Hart Crane, 'Hart' was his mother's maiden name. Grace knew that these two names would operate differently, suggesting two versions of the same man. The poet Eileen Myles imagines this decisive moment, around Hart's eighteenth birthday:

Hart Crane's mother came to visit from Ohio. And she talked a little about staying in New York, which must've been scary. Grace Crane in New York. Uh oh. Hart was *her* family name. He was Harold originally. That's who probably got the advertising job. C.A.'s son. Harold Crane. Why don't you call yourself Hart. Hart Crane sounds more like a real poet.

Myles speculates that it was Grace's idea to use a design by the painter Maxfield Parrish for her husband's candy company. I bet it was. On one of Parrish's designs for the company, a crane stands in a lake, its head dipped towards the true blue water, waiting to spear a fish, mountains in the background shaded in violet, lemon yellow and ultramarine. On the opposite side of the box is C.A.'s delivery truck, decked out in red-and-white candy stripes, there was a matching portrait of the bird painted on its side.

As I read the transcript for the second time, I could see Grace approaching her one-room apartment at 108 East 38th Street, Manhattan. In patterned brick, red at ground level, running to golden orange on the top floors, the building was raised in staggered blocks, up to the final yawns of the last three storeys, where a spacious duplex apartment stretched skywards. The tower that capped the building was illuminated by the afternoon light passing through the coloured glass windows that flanked the sides, each lidded with rainbow-painted terracotta panels.

It was the afternoon of 27 October 1940, two hours before a meeting with Frances, the medium Grace met through Christian Scientists. Grace was sixty-four. She was tall, and wearing a green wool coat in a straight cut with a subtle check and large lapels, held by one button at the left of her waist. The hem of her dress grazed her shins, a few inches beneath the coat in a matching shade, but with the addition of polka dots. On her legs were immaculate stockings and well-worn but neat laced black shoes. Grace could smell soot and car fumes, lingering tobacco and the hot bread in the groceries under her arm. She would rather have taken tea that afternoon. She could call down for dinner, perhaps. Though the prices were growing ridiculous on her salary. At her own restaurant, the Towne House, nestled in the apartment block where she was a housekeeper, it was now 35 cents for a lukewarm coffee and another 40 cents for a slice of pie. A diner would have to part with $1 for the omelette with duckling livers. Or $1.50 for the cold buffet: a bowl of julienned vegetables and a couple of transparent strips of ham. She felt a sudden and strange awareness of her body. The doorman could see her flesh rippling above her girdle, she was sure. He could see the skin compressing into wrinkles on the soles of her feet with each step. She flinched at his polite greeting and hurried to the lift, pained by the sound of her shoes on marble.

Upstairs, Grace took out a pile of notes – some handwritten, some typed. These were records of her meetings with Frances. A few of them would gather at the round table in Grace's apartment at the weekends, as they would that night. When it was just the two of them, Grace would make her way over to Frances's apartment at 1148 Fifth Avenue, a huge brownstone overlooking Central Park. It was a good hour's walk for Grace, but it saved her a few cents. If it was cold, she got the 4 or the 6, rattling through midtown on the subway, staring at the toothpaste and dandruff ads slotted above the lines of balding heads, headscarves, hats.

On her last visit to Frances – over a month ago now – she had left a little late. She hurried, the Chrysler Building on her right, stepping through the broad avenues until the park stretched forwards to her left. The Plaza. She had always thought it was a little tacky – the servers were over the top, managing to pour coffee in a way that seemed ingratiating. She eyed the women in furs as they spun in and out of the doors, nodding at the doorman. The streets were busy, with cars jamming against each other. Billboards advertised *Rebecca*, Cinzano in red, white, and blue, and a circus, just come to town. She hadn't seen the film yet – she might see if she could catch a matinee on her day off.

She was growing weary of the meetings, which descended into a series of lessons, where Frances would outline various stages of spiritual knowledge, the voice sounding increasingly divorced from her son's. Sat at her table, she took out last week's notes. The first line: 'Not a word will be wasted today'. Sometimes Frances would channel the spirits through the pen, drawing incomprehensible, vast shapes that had to be interpreted – looked at until the eyes crossed and a word or phrase, or sometimes just a letter, could be deciphered. Grace almost preferred those notes, teasing out or even inventing from the scribbles. She was using Hart's typewriter to turn the notes into a pamphlet. It was a Corona. Hart loved the music of the keys. She would deal with the most recent now, she thought, while there was still a little light. She laid out the pages from the last meeting and started work.

Frances arrived and they contacted Hart once again. The living room was flooded with candlelight, their hands clasped over the hardwood table. Her dead son reminded her that 'real ardor . . . includes sacrifice'. He gave them the title of a posthumous poem. They were writing it together, week by week. As 'Hart' communicated a new section of the new poem to Grace, she interjected: 'I wish you could come to me alone. I have been trying so hard to contact you. Won't you try to reach me?'

I see her in the darkness that night, tears pooling in her shadowed eyes.

3

Debts

From the carriage window, Hart watched the shifts in the landscape as the train threaded its way south from Veracruz. By now, the rats had travelled almost 2,000 miles, biting happily at the bars and whoever's coat covered their cage (Hart's, Zinsser's, Castañeda's). After five hours, the train pulled across the austere plateau beneath the city of Orizaba, flanked in the distance by rising mountains. The route was dotted with old walls, and the valleys were cut through with ledges that spilled with vegetation and bright flowers. At each stop, the three could buy fruit, tortillas, cake, serapes, beer and pulque – a drink made by fermenting the sap of the maguey (agave) – from stalls run by women at the sides of the tracks.

The train drew into Mexico City on 11 April, a Saturday. Postcards on stands showed a tourist's vision of the city. On one, a photograph of the Plaza de la Constitución (the Zócalo) from above. Built on what was once the ceremonial centre of the old Aztec city of Tenochtitlan, the square is bisected with wide walkways that bridge the ornate Catedral Metropolitana on the one side, and the Palacio Nacional on the other. The paths between the colonial state buildings form a cross, cutting through grass and palms. Other postcards preserved the view at ground level. Cars and buses unload tourists and pilgrims: a man runs, forever paused with his white trousers sailing out behind him. He overtakes a nun who, in turn, is captured at the moment she tilts her head to speak to her companion, with whom she walks arm in arm.

Hart headed to his hotel, assuring Zinsser and Castañeda that he would see them soon. Zinsser would be in the city for three weeks, and Castañeda through to July. Castañeda urged Hart to call him if he ran into trouble. 'If I ever get sick,' Hart explained euphemistically in a letter, 'he knows everyone from the president down.'

Hart's hotel, the Pánuco, was on the Calle Ayuntamiento, near the centre of the city. He slept, and woke with a sense of excitement and possibility. 'Am feeling as at the beginning of *The Bridge*,' he told his friend and publisher Caresse Crosby, 'only fresher and even stronger.' He hoped to recreate the artistic and intellectual communities that he had found in New York, Woodstock, and, briefly, Paris. He had arrived with an armful of letters of introduction from Waldo Frank to various officials, poets, and publishers. The Guggenheim Foundation too, he hoped, would bring him connections and routes into new friendships. The problem would be, as it always had been, navigating those new and fragile friendships through the jetsam of his erratic behaviour.

That Sunday, Hart wrote to Sam, by now an old friend, recording Zinsser and Castañeda's antics on the boat, and leaving out his own. His letter marvels in the Mexican landscapes:

the shapes created by the valleys and waterfalls, and the textures of the vegetation glimpsed from the train. Hart was always a prolific letter writer, but in Mexico he began to use his correspondence to preserve and explore his experiences, telling the stories of a handful of days hiking or at a festival at a fractionally different angle each time.

He stayed at the Pánuco for just under a week. From his room, Hart could walk to the Zócalo in around half an hour, where Diego Rivera was intermittently at work on *La Historia de México: de la Conquista al Futuro*, a vast mural on the staircase of the Palacio Nacional. Completed in 1935, Rivera's vast work illustrates Mexico's history, from Spanish conquest to the overthrowing of the Porfirio Díaz dictatorship during the revolutionary struggle of 1910–1920.

This way of painting – the vastness of its scale, with detail and panorama all at once – suggested new poetic structures to Hart. The Mexico poem could try to approximate a written form of these murals, with scenes duplicated and refracted, the panoramas of the landscape alongside fine detail. Through the rhythmic repetition of details, Rivera was able to mix the general and particular. Rivera includes a portrait of his wife, Frida Kahlo, but she takes on the part of mother-educator, dressed in a symbolic red that draws the eye up to a group of workers, a hammer and sickle flag, and Marx himself, holding the first page of the *Communist Manifesto* in Spanish. Perhaps Hart's half-started poem might have played similar games, lovers and friends at once precisely drawn and disguised in new roles.

On Monday, Hart walked to the bank. He collected his telegrams and began his calculations, scribbling numbers and lists in the backs of his notebooks by force of habit. The first instalment of his prize was almost gone, after paying off debts and a day or so of jubilant spending in New York. He had continued spending on the *Orizaba*. He owed Zinsser for expenses on board. Now he was waiting on a hotel bill.

Money was a constant source of anxiety. As a young man, Hart found himself caught between the financial wranglings of his divorced parents; his move to New York and living expenses had been a flashpoint for arguments in the last days of his parents' relationship, while Grace was frustrated with the settlement she received after their divorce was finalised. At sixteen and newly arrived in New York City, Hart wrote a begging letter to his father for 'necessities', emphasising that he had taken a 'too small' room. He confidently promised C.A. that in six months' time he would 'be able to stand on his own two feet'. This independence never fully materialised. Hart's ongoing appeals to his father for help were humiliating, and, until the last years of C.A.'s life, were generally dependent on promises to relegate poetry and writing to a hobby or secondary interest.

Although C.A. was wealthy, historically Hart had not been able to rely on him for support or without, for instance, promising to enrol in a local business school. To come to his son's aid would be to endorse his impractical ambitions. Hart had worked for his father on several occasions, starting (as C.A. had done) in a back room or delivering boxes of sweets. Hart records this in the poem 'Black Tambourine', when he was dismissed for ignoring the company's segregationist working policy, having been found in the break room designated for C.A.'s Black employees.

Hart had struggled to hold down jobs. In his twenties, he had some luck finding work in advertising in Cleveland and

New York, helped by his experience of selling advertising space for his father's chocolates in poetry magazines. Hart worked in various bookshops, including Sam Loveman's midtown store, as a shipping clerk, and had a very brief stint as a local reporter in his teens at the *Cleveland Plain Dealer*. For a long time, he had wondered how he might work at sea, perhaps as a ship's purser in the merchant navy, like Emil.

In 1930, Hart's prospects were increasingly hopeless in the wake of the 1929 crash. He was homeless. Hart drifted between the houses and hotel rooms of friends and lived in a tent in Patterson. He stayed with the poet E. E. Cummings and his then-wife Anne Minnerly Barton in New Hampshire for a spell, then moved between New York and Patterson. New York was difficult. He was trying to stay sober and the city pressed on him. As winter receded, he headed north: 'there is no liquor out here', he wrote. He arrived at Malcolm Cowley's property, where the two hooked trout and listened to the frogs' shrill singing in the marshes. The spring slowly arrived, heralded by the pussy willows and the stretching of light. A farmhouse in upstate New York could be held by deposit for $75. Hart had dreamed of that kind of security, convinced that owning a piece of land (even minus the house, for now) would bring him some ease.

When Hart had money, he spent it. He treasured a bronze cast of a seagull by the Paris-born sculptor Gaston Lachaise – a Patterson friend. The bird sleeps, its head turned and tucked beneath its wings. The sculpture recalls the seagull at the beginning of *The Bridge*. In the poem, the gull launches itself from the Gothic arches of the bridge as dawn breaks, its wings still 'chill' where it has roosted on the suspension wires for its 'rippling rest'. Lachaise's sleeping bird rests in the quiet before the start of the poem, which is ushered in by the gull's spring into flight, its 'dip and pivot' above the city.

In 1930, Hart earned just $350, supplemented with a $100 loan from his benefactor, Otto Kahn, and the occasional bung from his father. The $350 came solely from his writing: $150 from his publishers and $200 in prize money from *Poetry* magazine. This would have given Hart $29 a month, had he been able to ration it (this was roughly the budget needed for one week, scraping by). A furnished room in Manhattan cost $2–3 per week and a bottle of Gordon's $1.25.

Hart's friends stepped in where they could. He carefully recorded his debts in the same notebook he used to develop ideas for new poems. He had scrawled the word 'Precari' on the front page (Italian: precarious). There are the names of friends with the sum owed and a row of diminishing figures as Hart slowly paid off the debt. But alongside, Hart lists words, with a column of their spiralling associations: 'looted / the forfeit / disaster / forfeits and counterfeits'.

Financial danger felt imminent, even during Hart's moments of relative security, such as the Guggenheim, or his brief stints of employment with advertising agencies in New York in the mid-1920s. I discovered the depth of Hart's money worries soon after I first read his poems, taking out his letters and various biographies from the University College London library. Full-time employment meant that he had less time to write, but unemployment and financial uncertainty led to anxiety so crippling that writing became impossible. He finished *The Bridge* thanks to financial support from Otto Kahn. What he hadn't realised was that in accepting the money he had taken on a debt for life; it was not a gift. 'It seems I have to pay $60.00 odd the rest of my mortal term on life insurance to the Kahn estate', he wrote. 'I was dumb bell enough not to understand when he proposed it.'

I can't remember a time when I haven't worried about money, my hand on Mum's trolley at the grocery counter; praying my card will work one more time, tugging at the tatty neck of my sweater as I stared at the till. I am increasingly desperate to end my own interminable movement, first between degree programmes and then jobs, leaving one mould-ridden and damp rented flat for another. Each move requires sacrifice – forfeit, disaster – leaving behind friends, lovers, places: London to Oxford to Durham to Washington DC to Edinburgh to York to Maynooth.

In 2019, I had followed my Belfast-born boyfriend Karl to Kildare, where he was appointed to a five-year lectureship. After a year of part-time work at the nearby university, I accepted a job in Uppsala, Sweden, a city painted the toothsome colours of confectionery. For ten months, I abandoned the wooded square and blue-doored cottage where we lived, with its warm summer light that poured through a window in the leaves, shot through with lemon. I missed Karl and our dog, the nightly cloud of rooks, and the metre-long patch of inkcaps that, all through spring and summer, would appear overnight, melt, and return in an endless cycle.

I needed money. I finished my first degree in the midst of a recession, plunging straight into postgraduate study and then precarious, patchy academic employment. As a student, I worked at every imaginable job (fitting and selling corsets, waitressing, bartending, drawing fake tattoos on club goers, bookselling, college librarian). As a PhD student, I had the mild relief of a stipend, which provided just enough money to survive. I am sure that financial stability is a prerequisite for mental stability.

In Sweden I was working in a university on a short contract, ostensibly employed to teach American literature. More often than not, I found myself sat with teacher trainees discussing Dr Seuss, Katherine Rundell or Roald Dahl, imagining the perfect classroom for five-year-olds – I enjoyed this a great deal, though I was ill qualified to do it. The end of the contract loomed from the first day of the job and so my old financial habits remained. I knew I needed to save everything I could, preparing for my return to Ireland. I kept a fragment of paper on the fridge where I recorded every cent I spent. I hoped that this brief period apart might provide Karl and I with security in the future. Each day I arrived home to the tiny rented room and shrugged off my coat. I jotted down the day's total and lodged the pencil next to the hotplate. As I attempted to rectify the years of poverty that had left me with holed, worn clothes, I compensated heavily for any spending with long stretches of abstinence. I spent weeks living off cans of black beans; I had bought running shoes, a wool skirt, a warm coat.

In December 1930, Hart left behind New York and its bread-lines that snaked around several blocks, the rumours of men who had hauled themselves up flights of stairs just to step off the edges of buildings, the Hooverville shantytown, patch-worked from discarded wood and cardboard around the Central Park reservoir, crates of apples priced at 5 cents for the unemployed (one third of the city by that time). Hart was broke and exhausted. He took another job with his father. He worked at Crane's Canary Cottage, an old tavern in Chagrin Falls, Ohio, which C.A. bought in 1927. The building sat on sixteen acres, surrounded by woods. Many years before, Hart's grandparents had danced at the tavern during their courtship. Now the building functioned as a tourist attraction, with an adjoining shop selling C.A.'s confectionery.

Hart painted, polished and waxed the rooms and the elegant, plain wooden furniture. He greeted visitors and boxed sweets, securing Christmas-wrapped boxes with bows and stacking tins printed with the company logo's eye-catching white cranes. The cottage was the only arm of the business making a profit. Following the crash, C.A.'s wholesale business – his confectionery shops and restaurants – was in the red. If C.A. was concerned about his own financial situation, he shielded Hart from its severity. When C.A. died suddenly in 1931, just weeks after Hart's arrival in Mexico, the reality of what was once the Crane fortune was a shock. In 1930, at least, the three – C.A., his new wife Bessie, and Hart – were content together. Hart took a particular shine to Bessie, C.A.'s third wife, whom he felt had a mellowing influence on his father. She was just five years older than Hart and almost two decades C.A.'s junior.

Hart wrote to Sam: '*la vie sportif* continues its reckless pace hereabouts without any too great abundance of absinthe, gobs, apple-vendors or breadlines'. 'Driving in from the Falls, here, wrapping Xmas parcelpost bundles, and driving back at night, I lived in a veritable whirl of excitement', Hart told Sam. He joked that his improving health and small-town 'quietude' had bequeathed him a 'maidenly complexion and a bulging waistline'. Hart's drinking slowed and stopped. At Christmas there was turkey and all the trimmings, mince pies, expensive cigars, carols, brief calls to nearby friends and his aunt Bess.

At the Pánuco just three months later, Hart calculated what remained of his first stipend. He had $200 to last three months. And with that he would have to pay his hotel bill, rent a house, reimburse Zinsser. He had hoped to travel, hiking in the Sierra de Tepoztlán just beyond the city, exploring nearby villages and practising his piecemeal Spanish, acquired from books and dictionaries. Hart began to panic and sent a telegram to the local Guggenheim secretary, Eyler Simpson, a sociologist studying Mexico's agricultural communities.

On Tuesday afternoon Hart cracked and began to drink. Simpson arrived at the Pánuco and found Hart utterly drunk. He was kind, extracting Hart from his bedroom and offering him a welcome of sorts. They discussed Hart's projects, and Simpson promised to arrange an interview with Rafael Valle, the Honduran editor of Mexico City's paper *El Universal*. Talking to Valle soon afterwards, Hart explained his plan to write a 'portfolio' of 'song patterns' and 'dramatic cantos' combining 'symphonic voices' that would form sketches of the Mexican landscape.

Hart would have to reduce his spending immediately. He called a friend, the writer Katherine Anne Porter, who lived in Mixcoac, six miles out of the city centre. The two made plans. Hart would pack, settle his bill and leave the Pánuco early. He would stay a fortnight with Porter before heading into the countryside. Her patience was exhausted within a week.

4

Friends

Hart arrived in front of Porter's large, low house. A few streets away, the teenage Octavio Paz was reading in his grandfather's vast library. Octavio lived with his mother; his father, a Zapatista, had died during the revolution. Octavio was seventeen, and about to publish his first poems.

As a boy, Octavio heard the call to Mass from the twin bell towers of San Juan Evangelista and Santa María de Guadalupe, a sixteenth-century church with octagonal stained-glass windows. The Virgin of Guadalupe, who appeared four times to Juan Diego, an Indigenous Mexican peasant and convert, was carved into the space above the heavy wooden doors facing the street. From there, she watched over the parish and over Octavio – though he would soon renounce her.

Aged seventy-six, Paz – by now the great poet – remembered his childhood home in Mixcoac in his 1990 Nobel Lecture in Stockholm. The house was old and crumbling. As well as the library, it had a wild garden with pomegranate and fig trees and thorned bushes that scratched his legs. It was here that he first formed the 'emotional bridges in the imagination', as he called them, which linked him to the world and to others.

The bridges between us can be more or less real, more or less imaginary, more or less deliberate, accidental. For example, the teenage Hart Crane reads Walt Whitman's *Leaves of Grass* and he understands that the following lines address him directly: 'Whoever you are holding me now in hand . . . Carry me when you go forth over land or sea.' New friends – writers – meet in the New York offices of a literary magazine, or a bar, or the apartment of a mutual friend – they can't remember quite how it was. They meet again in another country, Mexico, and one offers the other lodgings. A thirty-one-year-old poet with a shock of silver-and-white hair and bloodshot eyes wanders the neighbourhood, photographing churches, violinists and cooks selling food in the street. Perhaps the poet walks past the house of the seventeen-year-old Octavio. Perhaps he brushes shoulders with Octavio in the street. The young Octavio flicks through a book written by an American poet. The poet had been his neighbour for a time. The poet had died as he made his way home. Almost sixty now, Octavio Paz translates Hart's last poem 'The Broken Tower', finished in Mixcoac. 'The bells, I say, the bells break down their tower; / And swing I know not where', wrote Hart. '¡Campanas, sí, campanas que hacen volar la torre! / Se mecen, no sé dónde', wrote Paz.

Paz's suburb was once an independent municipality. In 1910, the government opened an asylum in Mixcoac. Its doors opened to patients just weeks before the dictator President Porfirio Díaz was overthrown. Four years into the revolution it was occupied by the Zapatistas, Paz's father's group named after Emiliano Zapata, the leader of the Morelos people's revolution.

The Zapatistas fought the Constitutionalist army and laid siege to the capital. More recently, the writer Cristina Rivera Garza has spent years unearthing the stories of the inhabitants of the institution: Rosario E. who spent sixty years in solitary confinement; Modesta B. who may or may not have received diplomatic dispatches from the Bolsheviks and anarchists.

Now Mixcoac was being slowly absorbed by the southward sprawl of Mexico City, connected by wide streets with trams and motorcars. The houses there were generously sized. Porter had ten rooms, which were shared with her husband, Eugene Dove Pressly, a translator from Pennsylvania, and Mary Louis Doherty, an Irish-American working for the Mexican government and, for a short while, Hart. A long garden planted with fruit trees, rose bushes, nopales and palms stretched beyond the house. Porter kept dozens of animals. There were dogs, cats, turkeys, hens and a goat with golden eyes that nibbled at the pink rose flowers.

'The sun comes up warm from the edge of the morning, and the colors and smells and feel of the washed air are as near Paradise as I ever hope to come', wrote Porter to her father, describing the 'chill winds straight from the mountains' that blew through the city. In the mornings Porter immersed herself in a small pool that she kept ice cold. She dried off in the sun, bringing her kittens outside in baskets to join her. Then she gathered the avocados and figs that had fallen onto the lawn overnight before trying to sit down and write.

During these quiet mornings before the evening's parties began, Hart could be charming, doting even. Sam recalled how he liked to walk with one arm around his shoulder, a Whitmanian gesture, he explained. 'He would always grab you as a friend . . . he held on to you.' Hart and Porter would talk and work in the garden, weeding and planting out seedlings. Porter photographed Hart in one of these pleasant moments. Hart stood in front of a rosebush studded with new blooms, small and still folded into their centres. He bit his cigar, inhaling the smoke through his teeth. His grey hair, once the dark, reddish brown of stained wood, was combed behind his ears. Despite the heat, Hart wore a double-breasted naval coat and heavyweight Breton top. His white trousers were cinched with a recent purchase: a leather belt comprised of large pockets that circled the waist. He looked out of the frame and a grin formed around his eyes and mouth.

Porter's photographs of Hart connect five new friends: the photographer, her subject, and three others. Around Hart's neck hangs an 'ancient' silver pony bridle with jangling bells, a gift from the silversmith and collector William Spratling. One portrait was sent as a keepsake to Hart and Porter's friend Ernie O'Malley, the former IRA officer. Now a teacher, poet and art historian, O'Malley had begun a long exodus through Europe, the United States and Mexico in the wake of the Irish Civil War. The fifth: Moisés Sáenz, who introduced Hart and Porter to Spratling and O'Malley, worked in the post-revolutionary government as undersecretary of Public Education. And now I find myself drawn into the photograph's curious web: it arrives on my computer screen in an email from Ernie O'Malley's son Cormac, winging its way from Mexico to Connecticut to Uppsala.

Hart and Porter had first met in New York's Greenwich Village. Porter was born Callie Russell Porter in Texas. Her mother had died when Callie was just two. She was raised by her grandmother, living in various towns in Texas and Louisiana. After a violent, early marriage (for which she converted to Catholicism) Porter worked as an actress and a singer in Chicago. Then she began to wheeze. Her cough brought with it yellow-grey mucus: bronchitis. She spent two years in a sanatorium, emerging from its claustrophobic safety into the influenza epidemic. She was hospitalised once again. This time, her hair fell out. When it grew back, it was white. It remained so, throwing her striking bone structure into relief. Her face had the generously curved, connected shapes of a painter sketching on a table-cloth as a party favour: full brows sweeping around deep-set eyes, meeting broad cheekbones and a neutrally set, angular mouth.

Porter arrived in Greenwich Village in 1919. That year, the young Hart could be found in a frescoed building on West 16th Street. If visiting, Hart – not yet twenty – would appear hanging on the walnut banisters of the hallway in his slippers, tiptoeing through layers of dust, under chandeliers clinging to the crumbling ceilings and past the offices of an undertaker and the influential avant-garde literary magazine *The Little Review* (edited by sometime lovers Margaret Anderson and Jane Heap). The undertaker's stank: acrid chemicals filled Hart's bedroom as the morticians conducted their reverential and violent work, opening, stitching and preserving with the clack of a bottle lid, draining and pouring fluids and gently painting a jaundiced mask with the strokes of soft brushes, adding blush and darkening the lip and lash lines.

The bohemian atmosphere of Greenwich Village beckoned Hart and Porter from the Midwest and offered a haven for émigré artists. While there Porter became friends with the Oaxacan composer and musician Tata Nacho, and she collaborated with Mexico City-born painter Adolfo Best Maugard, also known as Fito Best. Artists like Nacho and Best made their way to New York for a host of different reasons: economic, political (as the revolutionary cycles turned), or simply seeking new audiences. The Whitney showed work by the political painter José Clemente Orozco and the sculptor Luis Hidalgo, who carved satirical forms of politicians, religious figures and matadors out of wax. Across town, the Guild Theatre showed a Mexican ballet. New York was experiencing an 'enormous vogue for all things Mexican', as historian Helen Delpar has written, culminating in the 1929 'Aztec Gold' exhibition at Madison Square Garden. It was a period of bilateral cultural exchange, pushed by both governments.

Working together in the theatre, Porter wrote pantomime scripts for Best, who designed and painted intricate stage settings for the performances. Porter and Best discussed his anthropological theories of art, mingling pre-Columbian traditions and contemporary experiment. Best painted portraits and landscapes that flattened the relief of a face, body or view into two-dimensional shapes. He surrounded these forms with intricate borders, adapted from the repeated patterns of Aztec design. If Porter moved to Mexico City, he explained, they might continue their work together, and she could pursue her growing interest in Mexican art forms.

Porter boarded a train at the United States–Mexico border in September 1920. She arrived in the capital in the wake of a new election, after the former President Venustiano Carranza had fled Mexico City with a large portion of the treasury and thousands of supporters, planning to set up an illegitimate government in Veracruz. Carranza was shot by rebels and, late in the year, Álvaro Obregón was elected – the first in a series of revolutionary generals to hold the presidency.

Porter wanted to capture the churning promise of post-revolutionary Mexico in her writing. The leftists of New York embraced the Mexican Revolution, but Porter had her own idiosyncratic reasons for her interest in the country's history. Her natural tendency towards rebelliousness and 'revolt' against a 'confining society' was at the root, she felt, of her fascination with the revolution.

Her sense of self was unstable. '[I have] the right to have changed my mind, my feelings and my point of view . . . Yet I am the same persons', wrote Porter. The plural was a fitting typo that inspired her next thought: 'I was at least two regiments of people inside, always at civil war.' She began to conceive of a series of stories that mapped the contours of the revolution – the country's reckonings with the long arm of colonial violence, and the more recent civil war – against more interior, psychological studies. Within a handful of weeks she had written 'The Fiesta of Guadalupe', taking the presiding saint of Paz's Mixcoac church as her first subject. In the story, she uses the Catholic symbol to explore social tensions within the new Mexico as the narrator attends the Feast Day, describing indigenous ritual dances and pilgrims stroking the cheek of the statue of the Virgin. The Virgin has 'grown accustomed to homage', she wrote, 'her eyes are vague and a little indifferent'.

Best introduced Porter to a large circle of friends in Mexico City, many of whom were major figures in the new wave of artists associated with the country's *Indigenista* cultural revolution. The movement asserted the need for Mexican artists to undergo a 'spiritual renewal', aligning their work with the pre-Columbian traditions of native painters and sculptors. Over the next decade, Porter's circle included fellow American, the photographer Tina Modotti, the muralists David Alfaro

Siqueiros and Diego Rivera, the painter Frida Kahlo, and members of their Syndicate of Revolutionary Arts, Sculptors, and Engravers.

She drank with the Soviet film director and theorist Sergei Eisenstein at a supper party and met Antonio Díaz Soto y Gama, a companion of Emiliano Zapata, who 'rode his mountains with his gang for seven years with a copy of Karl Marx and the Bible in his pocket.' She attended the Pan-American Federation of Labor Conference, danced at parties at the United States Embassy, visited the square-stepped Teotihuacán pyramids and, from an aeroplane, she photographed the smoke running off Popocatepetl, the volcano in central Mexico. In quiet moments at home she busied herself: she wrote, or she practised the same strains of Bach's preludes on her piano, over and over.

Soon she had an important commission. In 1921 the government organised Mexico's first folk art exhibition, Las Artes Populares en Mexico, which opened in the capital in September before travelling on to Los Angeles. Porter was asked to write an accompanying monograph, *Outline of Mexican Popular Arts and Crafts*, which would provide a key for the American audience. She found a seventeenth-century house in the city. She filled her room with gardenias. In the mornings, she woke to the sounds of baby parrots arguing over chunks of banana. They ruffled their bright green feathers with their beaks and moved across their branch in horizontal movements, half flying, half waddling, their heads turned in together in profile.

Rivera was nearby. Porter visited his studio often. She watched Rivera develop sketches into large-scale murals. Rivera had just had his first government commission for

Creation, at the National Preparatory School, alongside José Clemente Orozco and David Alfaro Siqueiros. He had painted a vast wall-space around the school's organ while Frida Kahlo studied in a nearby classroom – they did not meet until 1928. A large sun centres Rivera's composition. Its solar hands point outwards from the painting and into the school, beyond twelve-foot portraits of the Muses and Christian Virtues. Rivera spent a year working on the mural, constructed in a soft Italian style, with the paint applied in blousy-edged pastels.

Porter needed to educate herself, researching the traditions and construction processes of indigenous arts and crafts. She studied floristry, basket-making, woodcarving, intricately painted boxes, and Puebla pottery with 'Chinese blue on cream color, dragons and birds and leaves'. She marvelled at hand-stitched serapes and leather goods, with horse stirrups 'encrusted with silver flowers and leaves and birds'. 'In all these things,' she wrote, 'I have never seen two objects that bore the identical pattern.' Like many artists of her time, including Hart, she was wary of mechanisation and idealised their hand-made construction, noting that 'Every man makes a thing with his own hands, after his own thought.'

Hart acquired the hand-crafted pony bridle through a trip with Moisés Sáenz to his Taxco ranch, around 100 miles south of Mexico City. The bridle, Peggy explained, was a relic of the conquistadors, which did not seem to trouble Hart, who clasped it around his neck. Porter met Sáenz through Mary Louis Doherty and the three would ride out on long expeditions on horseback, exploring mountain villages. Sáenz, who Hart found 'daring' and generous, was an education advocate and reformer with a PhD from Columbia in comparative education. He was tasked with overseeing the expansion of schooling in rural areas in the Secretariat of Public Education. His aim was to promote the assimilation of Mexico's Indigenous population into broader society: both would need to be flexible, he decided.

Sáenz's Taxco ranch was close to Spratling's. Spratling, born in Sonyea, New York, settled in Taxco in 1929. He was introduced to Taxco by his friends Frida Kahlo and Diego Rivera. The two painters settled a little further north, taking a house in Cuernavaca the same year. Spratling's ranch was a sprawling, white-painted property with donkeys milling around the yard. The interior was a living museum, filled with ancient and fine rare silver. The rooms were lit with dozens of different lamps, hung at varying heights, and reflected in large bowls that Spratling hammered out of silver.

Spratling's designs made their debts to Mexican craftsmanship clear, making use of native gemstones and the rhythmic, striped patterns of Indigenous artists. He made earrings shaped like silver hands inlaid with azurite, positioned so that they reach around the wearer's head; a silver pitcher with the profile of an eagle; a frog ready to spring from the stem of a brooch pin. For Kahlo he made a heavy matching necklace-and-earring set: a thick collar of silver beads, woven to resemble chainmail, the earrings taking a segment of the pattern, hanging well below Kahlo's jaw.

Hart was lucky to have Porter's connections. While he had made two new friends on the *Orizaba*, Zinsser and Castañeda, the doctors would only be in Mexico City for a short while. He had arrived armed with letters of introduction from Waldo Frank to León Felipe Camino, the Spanish anti-fascist poet, and Genaro Estrada, writer, former ambassador and official in the post-revolutionary government. Hart was indifferent to Frank's friends, complaining of their lack of interest in 'anything indigenous'. Rather, they were busy 'aping' poets like Paul Valéry and T. S. Eliot. 'And they are all "bored"', Hart added. The 'great dinners' Hart imagined with the city's literary establishment did not materialise.

Joining Porter in 1931, over a decade into this new vein of her writing and research, Hart was full of the arrogance of a person entirely ignorant of their chosen subject. After reading Anita Brenner's anthropological study of modern Mexican art, *Idols Behind Altars*, Hart pompously declared his 'emphatic agreement with nearly everything said' – he had set foot in the country a matter of weeks ago. 'It would take me, I imagine, a long residence here to be able to contradict any of her statements,' Hart added. However, through conversations with Porter, Brenner (a Mexican Jew, educated in the United States), Sáenz and O'Malley, Hart slowly seemed to realise that he was a tourist.

Hart planned to explore the devastating period of colonial conquest in a new poem, beginning with the moment that Hernán Cortés sailed into Veracruz in 1519. In *The Bridge*, Hart revels in anachronisms, layering historical events in an imaginary present. At Hart's most idiosyncratic, Whitman appears to an aeroplane pilot and Rip Van Winkle wakes from his slumber in New York to sweep a tenement down on Avenue A. The fragments of the Mexico poem that he left behind suggest he had a similar idea in mind, mingling past and present. In the poem 'Havana Rose', the survival of the typhus virus (as Zinsser no doubt had explained to him) provides, through its infections over generations, a point of connection between the Mayans to Cortés to himself, Zinsser and Castañeda as they stand on the *Orizaba*, watching the rats drown.

Hart and Porter were both struggling to write. Porter had the germ of what would become *Pale Horse, Pale Rider* inside her, her masterpiece of three short novels. She was reflecting on the pandemic that she had miraculously escaped, with her white hair as a souvenir. She could blame Hart for her lack of progress. He made her sick, she said. He 'took her skin off'. Here was the 'roaring boy', who 'would laugh twice as loud, drink twice as much as everyone else' transplanted to her quiet house in Mixcoac.

Hart got on reasonably well with the visitors that milled in and out of Porter's house, but he disliked Pressly, finding him humourless and bitter ('sourish', he wrote). Unsurprisingly, Hart's dislike of Pressly was a source of tension between the two friends. Perhaps Hart was subconsciously attempting to replicate the relationships of his childhood, turning Porter and Pressly into caring mother figure and a distant father, and slotting himself between them. Uncomfortable, yet reassuringly familiar. He broke into the tranquillity of her home and destroyed it, Porter wrote. He was a changeling in her and Pressly's care, 'as if we had taken a human being into our lives and found it metamorphosed into a hyena'.

Writing in the 1960s, Porter took a dark view of her entire circle in Mexico City. Frances ('Paca') Toor, who edited the influential literary magazine *Mexican Folkways*, was 'unspeakable'. William Spratling was a 'fraud', Peggy Cowley, estranged wife of Malcolm, was 'awful', Hart was 'doomed and deviled'. Even Pressly was 'a kind of monster of indecision, self-pity, inertia, and gluttony'. As she would have it, her entire social group was made up of 'bloodsuckers', with herself as the exception.

Hart's appearance in Mexico City accelerated their friendship, artificially so. Proximity and a new environment can make for forced and ill-advised intimacies that are hard to retract. Even so, when Porter talked about Hart, she seemed to talk about herself. 'He said once that the life he was living was blunting his sensibilities, that he was no longer capable of feeling anything except the most violent and brutal shocks', Porter explained. But she too had, as she put it, sought adventure 'for the illusion of being more alive than ordinary'. Adventure has at its heart, she thought, the 'violence of motives, events taking place at top speed, at sustained intensity, under powerful stimulus and a wilful seeking for pure sensation.'

Porter admitted later that their friendship was built on a misguided superstition about 'the romantic irresponsibility of drunkenness'. For Porter, this provided a useful pretext for her writer's block. For Hart – who had recorded the mystical experiences he'd had while high in a dentist's chair in letters – it was a justification for his alcoholism. He might not have been drinking every day, but he drank when he was anxious (which was often), he drank when he was delighted, he drank when he was sad, to celebrate, commiserate. And when he started, he could not stop.

Living close to Hart for a fortnight, Porter recorded the sharp changes in his mood over the course of a day. He would wake cheery and relaxed, shifting into reflections on his behaviour. This drew him into a cycle of self-recrimination and back to the bottle with shame. When Hart starting drinking, he would begin to monologue, castigating himself. This cruelty, turned inwards, can be seen even in his earliest poems. His poem for Oscar Wilde 'C33' takes its title from Wilde's cell in Reading Gaol. The poem explores 'penitence', as Hart writes that 'needs bring pain' (to want is embarrassing, shameful). Elsewhere the imaginary disclosure of his homosexuality in 'My Grandmother's Love Letters' is met with 'gently pitying laughter' (both his own and his grandmother's simultaneously). He ridicules himself in 'Postscript' because, unlike Keats, he cannot make objects spring to life in his poems, as Keats seems to do in 'Ode on a Grecian Urn'. The urn in Hart's poem remains 'but marble', he complains, unmoving and without the layered meanings of Keats's ode.

During these evenings with Porter, Hart would grow increasingly distressed as he spoke, his anxiety rising uncontrollably. One night he began to cry and shout 'I am Baudelaire. I am Whitman. I am Christopher Marlowe. I am Christ.' But, Porter added, 'never once did I hear him say he was Hart Crane.' Humility is confidence, a belief in oneself that stands outside external validation. This kind of arrogance, with his greatness to be assumed through comparison, suggested a lack of belief in his own poetry, as Porter understood.

On Hart's final night with Porter, Hart ran out of his room onto the wide, flat roof. The moon was bright, illuminating his outline pacing above the group gathered below. He shouted. He threatened to jump. Porter responded with a tease: 'Oh, don't!' she said. 'It's not high enough and you'll only hurt yourself.' He laughed, and swung down an apricot tree close to the wall, landing on the grass. The anxiety that had forced him out onto the roof transferred its energies elsewhere. He talked too fast, too excitedly. He hammered on the out-of-tune piano. After an hour, he left in a taxi for the city.

5

The Towne House

Grace sat down, her legs heavy, and inspected her nails. She had spent the last of the evening wiping down tables. One or two were over-waxed (her fault) and the damp cloth kept catching on the translucent ridges that had bunched over the wood. The Christmas rush was over, but the restaurant needed to be perfect for New Year's Eve. There would be a big party. She didn't see the sense in it. 1941 would be just the same. She would scrape them down later.

Her cramped room was away from the guests, and accessible through a series of damp, hidden corridors. Still, it was better than the Carleton, where she essentially lived in a hole in the wall. She had stacked what remained of her possessions against the walls. The jewellery – the relics of marriage – was long sold, but two dresses that would never fit, but were so fine to look at, hung on the outside of the wardrobe door. She had pulled them out that morning, smoothing their rich fabric: tall columns of silk with trimmings that gathered in a tiny band at the top of the waist. Now she could barely step into them, the sleeves jamming on her forearms.

A few photographs stood on a dresser, centred on a picture of her son in some kind of white pyjama suit, looking morose with a frail moustache clinging to his upper lip. There were more in a box beneath her bed, alongside the gown she had worn on the night of her first marriage. She looked similar now to the way she did at twenty-two, when she first married. She was handsome, her dark hair pulled away from her face. Her strong jawline was only slightly weakened with age. She had on a long string of pearls and oval-shaped earrings, a light coating of lipstick and a light smudge of black around her eyes – just enough to define the outer corners. Her hair was set in careful waves, brought back from her tall fore-head. She still wore her eyebrows according to the 1930s shape – extremely thin and angled upwards at the bridge of her nose.

On the mantel above the fireplace she kept a bell – her mother's, used at school some eighty years ago. Elizabeth would gather the children around her with its rich sound. The children that were called to the sound of the bell must be dead now, Grace thought, and she tapped the warm metal with her fingernail, a low echo of its peal.

Grace stuffed the dresses back into the wardrobe. She could feel herself thickening. She stretched a hand as far as she could around the band of her skirt, measuring in an automatic move-ment. She left small indentations in her waist with her nails. As a girl, on good days she could place her hands below her ribcage, stretch them out and around and almost imagine them meeting. 'A daughter of steel,' she thought, laughing to herself as she resumed the inspection of her hands.

She eyed the guests below with a humour that was the close cousin of resentment. Her father would not have liked the Towne House. Certainly not the prices and the obnoxious spelling (the building was only eleven years old). The type of place that you visit because you can afford it, surging through the golden doorway, and not because it is good. She had tried the cakes – almost everything really, in odd bites – and they were bad. Too much marzipan, which the chef (who liked to read European books) insisted on grating into vast bowls from a large block. Everything in garish colours, too – hard, bright-coloured structures full of layers of over-whipped cream that stuck to her fork and furred her teeth.

These were fashionable when she was a girl. She had something like today's acid-green confection many years ago, back in Chicago. It was before C.A., she guessed, by a matter of days or weeks perhaps. The cake – a Princess cake – had been some kind of conciliatory gesture. She couldn't remember the details of the argument. Some sort of slight, a nasty comment, perhaps, or a forgotten invitation. But she recalled a hairless man slapping the domed cake down in front of a friend. It was an apology and a humiliation; the gift acknowledged the presence of a feud.

She had sung that night. A rangy man with hazel eyes had told her that she almost sounded Italian, stifling a laugh. She had seen him first, striding up the stairs towards her. He passed her on the landing, continuing into a loud room where he sat down. She pretended to pause to look at a painting. She heard a mess of sounds: screeching and lower rumbles of laughter, glasses clinking, fragments on the piano – it sounded like 'Break the news to mother', a war song. 'It was very convincing,' the hazel-eyed man said to her later, raising his thick eyebrows outwards. She enjoyed the smirk. Obvious disingenuousness was preferable to a man who was utterly sincere with you one hour, and utterly sincere with another woman the next. The man enjoyed contradicting the other guests, taking positions that he did not agree with and arguing for them forcefully. She had listened to him all night, her narrow back towards him as she nodded and smiled and pretended to pay attention to the circle in front of her: another party next week, a storm off Cape Ann, a drowning in the English Channel, blizzards in Boston, a fire in Connecticut, fruit imports to Germany were banned, a friend of a friend's suicide in Washington, yellow fever among the troops in Cuba, cheap loans in the city, for a time. One of these bores was going to make the most of them – real estate, a hotel, or something. 'Ah, my glass is warm,' she said eventually, 'I'll go and change it', and excused herself. She did not return, and instead sloped her arm around the shoulders of the pianist, whispering in his ear.

When she sang, she did not feel beautiful. Impressive perhaps, but ugly – neutrally so. She was – and she knew this to be true – unequivocally beautiful. Not the kind that required motion. She moved her head and body at careful angles as she spoke, catching the most flattering light and shadow. When she sang, she saw her nostrils flare and her body widen as she climbed the bars of the melody. Her ribs pressed against the taut fabric of her dress. She extended her hand, palm up, almost as if she was reaching to take fruit from a tree. That night she dreamed about hazel eyes. In the dream she was back at the party. This time, as he walked past her on the landing, he placed his hand against the velvet at the small of her back. She reached around behind her and held it there.

She had wondered, once, about acting. She used to practise gestures and expressions in the mirror, over and over, repeating lines from plays with her vowels clipped short. Some evenings, bored, she powdered her face until her features flattened, sketching in an artificial relief with rouge and fingers blackened with a candle wick. Being in California with Hart and her mother had been wonderful at first. She had only tried to help him, encouraging him to book meetings with agents, to hold himself in a certain way. He was always too sensitive, fixating on even the mildest of comments.

She ate something – a piece of bread (a little stale) and a wedge of cheese. She considered making tea, but decided to wait until all the small jobs were done. The diners had left. Back downstairs, Grace bent over the first of fifty tables. She chipped away at the varnish, pushing at the table with a knife until the sheen lifted in greasy scrolls. There were footsteps, and a round face appeared under a round hat. The new doorman was built all in circles. Even his shoes seemed to bulge. 'A letter, Mrs Crane,' he said (she had returned to her first married name after the second divorce). Honestly, why bother bringing them in to her? Grace paused her work for a moment and took the envelope. Sam's writing. She tossed it on the table.

A few days ago Grace had dinner with Sam and a new friend she had made from the building. Sam had directed a remark at the newcomer: 'I'm so glad that Grace has friends,' he had said. She scraped harder, her nails glancing the wood and debris bouncing onto the envelope. She had only sat with the woman once or twice. She had indulged her lively child, saving scraps for her in a napkin and closing her ears when she screamed and bounced around the table. Even now, days later, the memory was embarrassing. She would hate for the other woman to think she might presume their closeness. She tried to soothe herself in these moments, like you might a child, muttering under her breath and staring at the table below. They came at night, these blistering memories, comments that she filed away to inspect later.

She had scolded Hart when he cried. Or she laughed at him, finding his shame shockingly funny. Perhaps she was as cruel as her sister-in-law Bess had said. Or perhaps the child held up a mirror to his mother, showing the true scale and absurdity of her own anxieties. Once, when he was around five, he made a card for a woman who was a neighbour and walked over to what he thought was her house, his stocky little legs making purposeful steps. He held the card out in front of him like a beacon. Two sisters lived in the neighbourhood, and he delivered the birthday card to the wrong one. The boy retreated home, stuttering apologies between tears, his cheeks and eyes hot and his red hair mussed by his fretting hands. Grace howled over it for days. Her sister-in-law had never let her forget it – she told the biographer, too. People are such miseries. She had tears in her eyes for laughing. His heart had broken. It broke continually like hers.

She scooped the mess on the table into the front of her apron, walked across the room and tipped it into the fire.

6

Hart Crane's Flea Circus

Hart woke up in jail. His skin was itchy and sore with bites from the fleas that had made the old cell blanket their home.

He lies there, a prop in a travelling flea circus. The night before, the curdled morning, and the fleas all combine into a surreal pageant: 'Wahey and over the silver bridle I run and jump and! Fee fi fo the blood of a poet straight from his thumb!' the flea might have sung, dancing in a top hat. 'Friends! Am I elevated? Am I difficult?' the flea might have mocked, dots of blood at his lips. 'We had a cousin in Professor Bosco's with Chaplin's lads, who pranced, sprang from bowler hats, perched on moustaches and the wire batons glued to their bodies seemed to spin.' Then the fleas in chorus: 'Should we cry? *You could.* Did you see the others cry? *We did not.* What did you see them do? *They conducted seances: a bird flew around the room with sweets in its mouth. They prayed for the burning.* Should we turn out the lamps? *They are already low.*'

'I saw their teeth from the prow,' they murmur, as Hart made gentler sleeping sounds, 'hundreds of tiny teeth glinting yellow in the waves,' they whispered.

The events of the previous day were hazy, but set in a familiar pattern. There had been a row – a bill. Then the police. In Paris just a handful of years ago, his friend Harry Crosby had scooped him up in such moments. Harry had a word in the ear of the gendarmes of La Santé and sat in court as Hart waited to hear his fine, paying whatever was required. Then he took Hart, ashen-faced, for a pile of eggs and bread when it was all over, as morning turned into the afternoon and his hangover transformed into shame: coldness in the limbs, a grimace as memories intruded, the yellow yolks of the eggs suddenly disgusting, sulphurous yellow held together by thick ropes of glaire.

Harry was dead. Harry would have 'adored' Mexico, Hart told his widow Caresse Crosby, catching himself as he wrote about his friend in the past tense. But Harry had killed himself and he had killed Josephine Noyes Rotch, his lover, with a revolver in a New York hotel room at the tail end of 1929. It might have been a suicide pact, it might have been murder. The *New York Times* reported on the case with barely disguised excitement.

Harry's death was not a surprise. That he would take Rotch with him, though, was unthinkable. Like Ernest Hemingway and Archibald MacLeish, Harry was a volunteer in the American Field Service Ambulance Corps during the First World War. He was at Verdun and awarded the Croix de Guerre. Throughout the twenties, Harry planned for his death, which he felt was inevitable and looming. 'Let there be no mourning and lamentation', he wrote in a strange directive, which he printed himself using the signature black-and-red type of the press he founded in Paris with his wife Caresse, Black Sun. 'What ever have I had to do with lamentation', he added, thinking of Whitman, who wrote in 'Song of Myself' 'I keep no account with lamentation (What have I to do with lamentation?)'.

Together, Harry and Caresse had published D. H. Lawrence, Ezra Pound, Ernest Hemingway and Kay Boyle and, after Harry's death, *The Bridge*. As a teenager Caresse (known then as Polly) invented the modern bra. Frustrated with her 'boxlike', armoured, corset-manipulated silhouette as she dressed for a Manhattan ball, Caresse sewed a pair of handkerchiefs and a pink ribbon into an ingenious, supportive garment. Her design, the 'corselette', was patented in 1914. 'I can't say that the brassiere will ever take as great a place in history as the steamboat, but I did invent it,' she wrote later.

Approaching her fortieth birthday as Hart sailed out to Veracruz, Caresse had just bought a clipper. Writing to her from the *Orizaba*, Hart applauded her decision to swap Paris for the sea and sighed that he would miss one of his own 'proverbially good sailors' after rerouting his fellowship from Marseille to Mexico. Hart's fascination with sailors was an open secret among his friends (there was Emil, another called Jack Fiztin, Bob 'Tuscaloosa', 'Circe', a red head in California). Sam called it a 'fetish'. Rizal Gaultier thought of Hart and sailors simultaneously, asking Sam, 'Have you seen Crane? Every time I see a sailor I think of him.' In this case, the sailor in question was K. Peter Christensen: 'my sweet tall boyfriend who you met more than once', he reminded Caresse. Perhaps she might consider employing his lover on her boat, he added, enclosing a photograph of the handsome Dane.

After Harry's death, Caresse coaxed Hart through the

painful final stages of work on *The Bridge*. The edition was also a memorial. Harry had loved the poem. He read the new sections as Hart finished them, high on opium pills (his 'black idols') and marvelling at the sounds echoing and knotting around each other: 'teased remnants of the skeletons of cities', 'dreams wreathe the rose', 'A wind worried those wicker-neat lapels'.

Caresse put her energies into assembling *The Bridge* for publication. She arranged Walker Evans's photographs so that the suspension wires seem to flee the square pages. Hart, meanwhile, wrote an elegy for Harry, 'To the Cloud Juggler'. Hart writes for his friend:

> Wrap us and lift us; drop us then, returned
> Like water, undestroyed, – like mist, unburned . . .
> But do not claim a friend like him again,
> Whose arrow must have pierced you beyond pain.

Hart conjures one of the greatest elegies in English here, Milton's *Lycidas*, written in 1637 for the death of a fellow Cambridge student, lost at sea. Milton enters Hart's poem through the details of language, with Hart borrowing his characteristic use of the 'un' prefix (these have been counted by some patient soul, with almost a thousand of them in *Paradise Lost*). This grammatical structure holds up the thing being conjured for view even as the poet tries to negate it. It turns a word upside down. The painful idea is held in mind, even as it is being denied: *un*burned, *un*destroyed. We do not, of course, think of wholeness or intactness here, but the acts of burning, destruction. A synonym without the negative prefix (such as intact) would not have the same effect.

Upending language suits the movements of the elegy. An elegy is a poem for the dead, or for the consolation of those left behind. But it finds its energy in the inherent embarrassment or problems of this conceit. It is effectively mourning as self-fashioning, using the occasion of a death to say something about oneself. An elegy addresses those left behind ('do not claim a friend like him again'), while also performing rites of mourning. For Classical poets, the elegy was a necessary genre for a poet to conquer to advance their career, as Milton knew and emulated. And so the elegy turns inwards, dramatising the writer's own grief, or the performance of it. Guilt accompanies this action, as the writer makes art out of death and sorrow. 'Is it craven?' asks Milton, as he gathers himself in the opening lines of *Lycidas*: 'I come to pluck your berries harsh and crude, / And with forc'd fingers rude'. '*Write* it!' Elizabeth Bishop commands herself in 1976 in the final line of her elegy 'One Art', as she forces her own hand.

Hart's skin was aflame and Harry was dead. 'It is blood to remember; it is fire', he admitted in *The Bridge*. The events of the previous night were a mess, but a thread could be detected as he lay on the floor, grateful for the cold stone. He had threatened to jump off her stupid, low roof. Porter had laughed at him. He had clowned down the apricot tree, continued the performance by thumping on the piano. He could not call her, surely.

Hart rang the American Embassy at 9 a.m. A Mr Aguirre answered the telephone. He listened and wrote down Hart's account in a record book. Hart explained that he was an American citizen, and that he had failed to pay a bar and taxi fare (2.30 pesos in total). Mr Crane was to remain in jail until noon, when a judge would set an appropriate fine.

After Hart put down the first call, he contacted the Guggenheim Foundation. Perhaps he hoped to improve his circumstances by leveraging the prestige of his award. All it did, though, was earn him a reputation with his benefactors as a drunk – and a dangerous one – resulting in the near-cancellation of his fellowship.

After the familiar ritual (judge, fine) Hart was free to leave. He needed another drink, and headed to the Mancera, Zinsser's hotel. The Mancera was built in the colonial style, with an ornate facade. It advertised itself modestly ('A good hotel with moderate fees'). Hart sat down in a bar decorated in a mixture of styles: art deco and traditional, with geometric patterns on the floor, carved vegetation on the mouldings. The drinkers and diners were separated by wicker screens and a tall, broad palm in a golden planter.

Zinsser allowed Hart to run up his tab. Zinsser explained this decision in his biography, offering a sanguine diagnosis of Hart's condition: while he had tried to help Hart cut down his drinking, it was ineffective and seemed to increase his depressive episodes. Instead, Zinsser opted for damage limitation; allowing him to keep a tab at the Mancera might at least help keep him physically safe and out of legal trouble for the duration of his research trip.

Hart drank all afternoon. In the evening he returned to Porter's. He felt unwell. The small bumps on his body and face had expanded with scratching into painful welts and a flurry of stress hives had bloomed on his neck and shoulders. Porter tried humour again. She joked that perhaps Hart had acquired a dose of syphilis on his most recent outing. Why not add Lysol disinfectant to the bath, she said, half serious, referring to futile attempts to treat the disease before the discovery of penicillin.

Hart, who had suffered the homophobic comments of friends for years, did not see the humour in Porter's suggestion. He was terrified of rejection, and the prospect simmered in even his closest friendships. Susan Jenkins Brown, whom Hart considered a dear friend, offered one of many cruel summaries in her book *Robber Rocks*: 'he never completely gave up the struggle against his two weaknesses, alcohol and homosexuality.' Allen Tate wrote that Hart's 'monstrous egotism' was 'grievously aggravated by homosexuality', describing him as 'an extreme example of the unwilling homosexual'. I am reminded of the calling card left for Oscar Wilde at the Albemarle Club in London by John Sholto Douglas, the Marquess of Queensberry: 'For Oscar Wilde posing Somdomite' [sic]. 'Posing', 'unwilling'. This missive prompted Wilde to sue the Marquess. The result of the two following trials was Wilde's own imprisonment for 'committing indecent acts' with men. He was consigned to hard labour, sorting the threads of heavy naval ropes and walking a penal treadmill – the state's machinery of atonement. His health failed and he died in Paris in 1900, three years after his release. 'But you who hear the lamp whisper through night', Hart writes in 'C33', imagining Wilde in his cell. The lamp light is oddly unseen, but it is heard as the sound of its guttering forges a path 'tear-wet' between the Reading cells and between Wilde and his queer readers.

The poet Marianne Moore viewed Hart's sexuality as a 'Decadence' that emerged in his poetry. It was, for her, the source of its collapse. After Hart's death, Porter is recorded as saying, close to tears, that Hart could have been a great poet, had he 'controlled his life, and not have given way to the vices of alcohol and sex'. In a book of conversations with Porter conducted decades later, she made the disturbing claim that

Hart smuggled 'boys' to his room, forcing 'his perversions' on them. This claim is unverified. I could not find substantiating evidence in any of Hart's letters, Porter's letters at the time, or those of Hart's friends and contemporaries, while they are all awash with jokes and careful revelations about sailors and other male lovers. What I do know is that Porter was disgusted by Hart's homosexuality. Homophobes have long weaponised the very real trauma of abuse against the queer community (take, for examples, charges of grooming against drag queens, a favourite topic of the American Family Association). In Porter's mind he was decaying, degenerate. Whatever the tenor of the Lysol joke, prompted by Hart's painfully marked skin, perhaps his reaction was fuelled by a broader context of rejection and insult from his friends.

Years later, Porter admitted that she had, on occasion, deliberately needled Hart. But, as she explained of his rapidly changing moods, she 'wished to repay brutality with brutality'. Sam and Hart, too, had begun to argue over his drinking. According to Sam, Hart increasingly began to believe that his writing and drinking were inextricable – that he could not write without it.

Hart did not notice, perhaps, the ways that the long spells of writer's block seemed to map onto drunken episodes, where frenetic evenings led to words becoming fewer and further apart. I have lived close to alcoholism, to an alcoholic writer. I have arrived home from work to find him apparently – but not – dead, a phone going silent overnight before a call from the hospital, outrageous and incomprehensible arguments. It is a deceitful disease, infecting every party involved. There was a tiring and daily fixation on avoiding alcohol, secretly pouring it down the sink or, at Christmas, into a pan of gravy, overboiling the liquid until I felt it was safe. Mercifully, I have also lived close to recovery. Each line is a triumph against the disease, rather than written in its debt.

In this case, the two writers traded humiliations. Hart packed and stood outside her gate. He screamed at her from the garden: she was a 'fancy man', 'a whore', a 'fancy woman', he shouted, before leaving. Hart returned to the Mancera, continuing the argument with a telegram while he was still half cut:

NO. HAVEN'T BEEN BUSY WITH 'LOVERS'. JUST YEOWLS AND FLEAS. LYSOL ISN'T NECESSARY IN THE BATHTUB. HAVEN'T GOT 'ANYTHING' YET. IF YOU KNEW ANYTHING WHATEVER ABOUT IT, YOU'D KNOW THAT AT LEAST (AND THE LAST THING SYPHILIS DOES) IT DOESN'T ITCH. OTHER MATTERS DO, SOMETIMES.

He would need to find somewhere else to stay.

7

The IRA Officer

I was sitting on the long, golden torso of a reclining man. He had laid down at the side of the Fyris, a river that runs through the Swedish Uppland through to Lake Mälaren and which takes its name from the tenth-century battle of Fyrisvellir, recorded in the Norse sagas. The man was naked, his arms clasped behind his head, hands securing triceps. I was perched on his ribs, his pelvis and the suggestion of a dick to my left, followed by taut legs that stretched him out to ten feet. Thanks to the ingenuity of Swedish design – at once completely mad and completely practical – the man was heated to body temperature with a device hidden somewhere beneath the metal. He left a melted rectangle in the deep snow around his frame. I could feel the warmth of him through my gloves, legs and arse. The heels of my boots sounded hollow against his golden body as I swung my feet.

I had walked from my tiny apartment down to the river in the day's slim tranche of sunlight. We were edging towards the equinox, and the gap was narrowing quickly. Soon the sun would set before three in the afternoon. It would be dusk all day, the sun barely dragging itself up in the mornings before its fall. It was 2021 and my first winter in Sweden and, as it transpired, my last.

A colleague had urged me to welcome the darkness and the cold. And so at 6 a.m. I lit candles at my desk and shook spices into my coffee in the morning and drank liquorice tea in the afternoon. I continued to run even as the temperatures dropped, lacing up obnoxiously orange trainers made for ice and snow, wrapping my head in a merino scarf, and clipping myself into a vest studded with flashing lights. I would set out in the dark, following the Fyris down towards the lake. It was silent, save for the crunch of my shoes and the slice of bikes passing, their studded tyres gripping the ice, lights cloudy and glowing through the falling snow. The river was frozen, glazed with a thick layer of snow. Occasionally I would see footprints across it, close together or long, exploratory slides – both kinds looked like dares or chances.

I had sat down on the golden man on my way to find somewhere to settle for a coffee, to be comforted by the incomprehensible chatter in the city's vast cafes. My favourite occupied a series of large rooms, dimly lit with candles and decorated with gilt-framed mirrors and antique chairs upholstered in old and beautiful silk fabrics. These stood in clusters around large, briskly polished wooden tables in every shade of oak and mahogany.

I had a copy of Ernie O'Malley's first memoir in my bag, which he started in the weeks before he met Hart. I was trying to puzzle out their intense friendship, and why O'Malley had made his way to Mexico from Ireland, where he was a veteran of the revolutionary struggle and the Civil War.

O'Malley wrote his memoirs from this position of exile. Like Hart, Ernie was peripatetic. He left Dublin early in 1925. It was a long exodus – ten years. On foot, he made his way through Italy, France and the Pyrenees. In his archive in New York I came across his counterfeit British passport, necessary for his travels. He gave himself the name Cecil Edward Smyth-Howard and lists his birthplace as Winchester, the closest city to the village where I spent the latter part of my childhood. Other details in the passport were true and partially true: that he was a medical student (he was, on and off), that he was five foot eight, grey-eyed, and with fair (red) hair.

O'Malley was part of Ireland's revolutionary struggle and the Civil War that followed. The touchpaper was lit during the 1916 Easter Rising, while O'Malley was in his first year as a medical student at University College Dublin. The Rising was followed by the War of Independence, fought between 1919 and 1921. In December 1921, representatives of the Irish Republic and the United Kingdom of Great Britain and Ireland signed the Anglo-Irish Treaty, ending the war. The terms of the treaty meant that Ireland would operate as a self-governing dominion of the British Empire. It also effectively led to the partition of the island. The British insisted that the six north-eastern counties could opt out of the Irish Free State – which the six duly did. The monarch would be the head of the Irish Free State, to whom members of the Oireachtas would have to swear an Oath of Allegiance. For some, the treaty was pragmatic. For some, like O'Malley, it was unconscionable. The revolutionaries split into two camps: pro- and anti-treaty.

Civil War broke out the following June, lasting just under a year. Its murmurs began in April 1922, six years since the

Easter Rising. O'Malley's garrison of anti-treaty Republicans occupied the Four Courts, housing the upper tiers of the Irish legal system. Free State forces laid siege, led by Michael Collins. On the last day of June, a final round of explosives blasted through the stone walls, forcing the anti-treaty rebels to surrender. O'Malley was captured and taken to the Jameson distillery around the corner. He escaped and headed south, making his way through Wicklow to Carlow. He was captured once again in November and taken to Mountjoy Prison. O'Malley was lucky to survive. The other IRA leaders present at the Four Courts were summarily executed: Rory O'Connor, Liam Mellows, Joe McKelvey and Richard Barrett.

O'Malley's numerous escapes from the British and Free State forces are easy to romanticise. I did this myself, sat on the golden man, clumsily thumbing the book and imagining O'Malley running through the Wicklow Mountains, dust lingering on a woollen jacket, tar peaks smudged green and purple. But O'Malley instinctively knew that romanticism was dangerous. He was wary of 'developing into a symbol', as he put it in a letter, hearing his name slip into songs about battles played in dances out in the countryside.

And so he left Ireland. Years later, he confessed that he was avoiding the trauma of the preceding years. The 'associative' memories 'intrude too much at home', O'Malley wrote, finding solace in the 'impersonality and detachment' he felt while travelling, living briefly among different communities. And leaving opened up the possibility of writing. He began to consider a memoir. He wrote two, *On Another Man's Wound* and *The Singing Flame*, in which he remembered the revolutionary and civil wars, respectively. In both books he looks back at Ireland from the Americas, signing his preface to the first volume '1931–34, New Mexico, Mexico, Peru'.

It is tempting to find O'Malley in lines from one of the plays that kept him company on his travels, Lady Gregory and W. B. Yeats's *Cathleen ni Houlihan*, which debuted a few weeks before his fifth birthday. In this one-act play, Cathleen ni Houlihan, first played by Maud Gonne, delivers a prophecy of sorts. She is free Ireland personified, transformed into an old woman. Arriving at the doorstep of a family celebrating the marriage of their son, ni Houlihan tells the family that she requires the defence of her lands. This is to be an ongoing sacrifice, she intimates: 'many that have been free to walk the hills and the bogs and the rushes will be sent to walk hard streets in far countries; many a good plan will be broken'.

O'Malley's body bore the marks of the last decade. He wore special boots, designed to accommodate injuries inflicted by British torturers in Dublin Castle as 1920 turned into 1921. 'I learned to walk again in the Pyrenees', he wrote. Six bullets had made his flesh their home, and there they remained until his death in 1957. The six were shot from the guns of Free State forces in November 1922, during O'Malley's capture.

Plans were broken, far countries were walked through. In Mexico, O'Malley met Hart Crane. Ernie wrote to the poet and editor Harriet Monroe, a mutual acquaintance (really more of an antagonist of Hart's) to explain their connection: 'we became friends and remained friends to the end despite my sense of personal discipline and his utter lack of it'. An illustrative example: on hunger strike in the last days of 1922, O'Malley read recipes aloud to his cellmate, George Plunkett, believing that he must directly face the process of starvation.

83

If O'Malley is left as a caricature of military asceticism, his friendship with Hart seems baffling. But O'Malley's writing, correspondence, and the objects and documents in his archives show his complexity, with deep interests in art, literature and folklore. These passions were linked by a fascination with how we tell stories, weaving together history, testimony, and legends in his public and private writings. His notebooks are stuffed: two rows per line in a near illegible hand with his observations ranging from Yeats, Lady Gregory, Gertrude Stein and D. H. Lawrence to architectural principles and, with sketches, the proportional rhythms used by painters. He collected paintings, paying in instalments where necessary for works by Jack Yeats, where figures emerge through thick layers of paint and colour; photographs by Paul Strand and Edward Weston; a conical sculpture of a head, eyes closed, by the Czechoslovakian Mayo-based sculptor Gerda Frömel; prints by Rockwell Kent; figurative sculptures by Native American artists Nina Rodriguez and Julian Martinez.

In the 1930s, O'Malley preserved oral histories for the Irish Folklore Commission in his native Mayo, gathering stories from Clew Bay and spending long nights listening and scribbling in his impossible, slanting hand. He knew that the move from an oral to a written artefact was a troubling but necessary compromise. As Walter J. Ong writes, 'thinking of oral tradition or a heritage of oral performance, genres and styles as "oral literature" is rather like thinking of horses as automobiles without wheels'. Through interviews conducted with former soldiers, he meditated on how we record and understand the past, preserving the testimony of dozens of former IRA Northern Division members recounting their experiences of the Civil War. Ensconced in these conversations are nested stories, where interviewees shared second- and even third-hand tales, preserved by O'Malley: 'A sergeant, a northerner, told me a story', 'He was a tailor in Musgrave Street and there's a story about that.'

Hart and O'Malley both write the past and present in messy, sheer layers. Hart has Helen of Troy waiting in traffic in a streetcar in 1920s New York. His Walt Whitman walks 'the beach / Near Paumanok' into 'infinity'. Emily Dickinson and the modern dancer Isadora Duncan, who were only briefly alive at the same time, in Hart's imagination hear and respond to the same 'stilly note' of the Angelus. O'Malley begins *On Another Man's Wound* with the memory of his nurse telling the stories and legends of Fionn mac Cumhaill, Cúchulainn, and Ferdia of Connacht, and how she sang ballads like 'Siúil a Rún' ('Go, my love'). Later, a faded green hat invites the story of how twin bullet holes were made on either side of its crown. A pair of boots prompts memories of long stretches of walking and leaping across ditches. He was sceptical of institutional history, with narratives decisively shaped by colonial powers. And so he was sensitive to the slippages between the self and others, between authoritative history and folklore. 'The dead walked around', he writes sincerely of ancient folk tales on the Rosses, 'the wall was thin between their living and their dead.' It is a book that plays with the boundary between fiction and history, how we write stories, and how we might write about ourselves between the individual and institutional histories.

In a 1935 letter to his then-fiancée, the American artist Helen Hooker, O'Malley explained how he was trying to piece together an archaeological map of Ireland. With skills accumulated from visiting excavations in Mexico, he hoped to record the complex archaeological layers of each county. It was just months before they would marry in London, so he swore that he would pause his investigations until they were together. 'I want', he told her, 'something that is of your blood and bones.'

Hooker's photographs are astonishing. Mirroring O'Malley's hopes for his map, they capture long traditions and practices, making layers visible. Taken in 1938: spectators at Carrowmore walk out across the low-tide sand to watch horse racing, seeming apparitional; on Clare Island, a crowd clusters on a bank for an annual regatta, a lobster fisherman sits outside a house, his intricate wool jumper split at the neck from wear; the ribcage of a currach on Inishbofin, a tangle of oars balanced between a seat and the lip of the boat.

Hart became a ghostly presence in O'Malley's writing. In *The Singing Flame*, published after Hart's death, O'Malley conjures a poem by his friend, lost years ago. Lost too, O'Malley thought, were the poems Hart had entrusted to him. In the book, O'Malley remembers the slow bleed of spring into summer during the opening salvos of the Civil War. When the Free State forces turned the walls of the Four Courts to fragments of stone and powder, they also destroyed the Public Records Office in the adjoining building. O'Malley recalls the moment that documents dating from the twelfth century were lost: 'The yard was littered with chunks of masonry and smouldering records; pieces of white paper were gyrating in the upper air like seagulls . . . Flame sung and conducted its own orchestra simultaneously.'

Hart's 'To Brooklyn Bridge' can be glimpsed in O'Malley's elegy to the lost archives. In Hart's poem, a seagull circles the 'chained bay waters' of Manhattan. Its wings are 'apparitional' as 'some page of figures to be filed away', ghostly records or scraps of paper that vanish, and with 'inviolate curve, forsake our eyes'. Hart's seagull takes off, springing from the bridge and beginning the poem. Papers fly and O'Malley surrenders his group of soldiers, under instruction by his IRA commanders. Papers burn and a three-day-old war beds in for a year. He is imprisoned. He escapes. His comrades are shot. He is imprisoned again, released long after the conflict was over.

O'Malley and Hart had writer friends in common, or at least overlapping circles from Hart's time in New York. O'Malley had arrived in Mexico via Mabel Dodge and Tony Lujan's house in Taos, New Mexico. Behind the house was the Sangre de Cristo mountain range. Bought in 1917, Dodge's twelve-acre home replicated her old salon in New York, providing a space for artists to meet, in large part for her own entertainment. The construction of the Dodge house was guided by her friend and future husband, Lujan, a leader of the Tiwa Puebloans. Adobe clay formed rounded and stacked shapes, burnt orange walls were accented with window recesses painted turquoise.

Many writers and artists were drawn out to the West with the promise of reduced living costs. In 1924, D. H. Lawrence and his wife, Frieda, bought a ranch close to Dodge and Lujan. After Lawrence died in 1930, he was turned into a block of concrete. His ashes were mixed with cement, weighed down with stones, and set down in a chapel in the mountains. Among Dodge's moths was the Antrim-born poet-mystic and IRA gunrunner Ella Young. She saw ghosts and heard fairy song. On Achill Island Young heard spectral music, a 'running crest of melody like foam on a sea-wave or moon-gilding on the edge of a cloud', 'a snatch of a song' with 'the resonance of a swung bell'. Later in the 1930s, Georgia O'Keefe – Hart's friend

– moved to Taos. She painted the landscape that surrounded her Ghost Ranch. She looked out on green cedars and, behind them, pink-and-yellow cliffs and flat-topped purplish mountains. O'Malley, too, tried to capture something of the landscape in poems, getting at the interplay between natural and built structures in the area's indigenous architecture, where he saw 'mountain shades' 'outstretched' into the 'angles' of houses.

Drawn further south by the post-revolutionary art scene that wove indigenous art forms with modernist experiment, O'Malley crossed the border with two artists, Theodora Goddard and Dorothy Stewart. The group formed in Santa Fe, New Mexico, with O'Malley employed to drive the two artists to Mexico in a borrowed car. The trio arrived in December 1930, their friendship preserved in letters home co-written and illustrated by the group. Stewart – whose great love was Maria Chabot, Georgia O'Keefe's assistant and lover – sketched O'Malley. His aquiline nose, round glasses, coat and an abandoned cup are gathered with a few exuberant lines as her friend intently reads the paper.

O'Malley and Hart met through Sáenz and Porter's circle. O'Malley was a teacher, spending time visiting rural teacher-training schools, through which he probably met Sáenz. As a teacher, O'Malley sounds uncompromising, even perversely ambitious, covering Schopenhauer, Shakespeare and history via D. H. Lawrence. O'Malley spent his spare time immersed in archaeological research in the Academy of Fine Arts, a decade later producing a broadcast *Traditions of Mexican Art* for the BBC's Third Programme. He had acute insights into the art of muralists Diego Rivera and José Clemente Orozco, admiring Rivera's 'colour, a grand sense of design' and the 'steel-like quality' of Orozco's treatment of indigenous subjects.

In Mexico City, O'Malley spent time exploring local arts, viewing frescoes and visiting libraries. He drank tequila and read Chaucer, worrying that 'Lack of the language keeps me from going any deeper into the life, the life so vibrant and intense. I am on the surface, a damned dilentanti – or however it's spelt.' He shared this frustration with Hart, whose Spanish was rudimentary. Both were frustrated with their writing projects, with O'Malley complaining about 'the damned book on which I am not able to do anything'. The more Hart learned about the country, the more he realised the scale of his proposed project, and his arrogance in thinking he, a poet from Ohio with barely a word of Spanish, could take it on.

Hart and O'Malley spent their time drinking and discussing poetry and paintings. Hart wrote excited letters describing his new friend: 'I have the most pleasant literary moments with an Irish revolutionary, red haired friend of Liam O'Flaherty, shot (and not missed) seventeen times'. O'Malley was 'the most quietly sincere and appreciative person, in many ways, whom I've ever met . . .' Hart wrote, 'we drink a lot, look at frescos – and aggree! [sic]'.

O'Malley partially registered Hart's problem with alcohol. 'Hart is a hard drinker: fifteen litres of beer the other day then I passed out', O'Malley wrote in his diary. O'Malley stayed for weekends with Hart in Mixcoac, on a bed borrowed from Porter, and the two spent giddy evenings together, drinking rum toddies and writing long letters to poets that they would never send, burning them in the early hours. In their sights: E. E. Cummings, Wallace Stevens.

O'Malley's deep interest in the muralists found its way into 'Nopal', one of the sheaf of poems that Hart entrusted to O'Malley. Three years after Hart's death, O'Malley recalled

Hart's reasons for passing them on to him: 'He said they were for myself as I had stood by him in trouble.' O'Malley sent them back to Ireland along with a few books, and was convinced the entire set had been lost.

After I came across 'Nopal', I wrote to O'Malley's son, Cormac, for help in verifying the poem. A few days later (by chance, on the eighty-seventh anniversary of Hart's death), Cormac responded with a beautifully detailed analysis of the paper and typefaces in his father's archive, confirming Hart's authorship. The poem addresses the *Opuntia* cactus, or prickly pear, and must have been written at some point in May or June, after the two had met, but before Hart's brief return to Ohio after the death of his father in July 1931.

Hart's conversations with O'Malley bear their traces on the poem. The poem presents a critique of colonialism that seems to borrow from his revolutionary friend – at a far remove from his thoughtless use of Native American history in *The Bridge*. In 'Nopal', Hart writes:

> Outfaced and in, a mirror, section-burnt,
> Distorting images recessed in angled green.
> Edge stabbed and pricked, bayoneted by sun.
> Upthrust and out; in rage, despair or what?
> Sucking cool sweetness from the heat lashed sand,
> Dribbling weak blood from out of bird pecked tunas
> And armed with a desert disregard.

It is a slight poem, but it does show the new directions of Hart's poetry. The infinite recessions of the nopal in a mirror suggest Hart's interest in Mexican history. He was fascinated by Anita Brenner's examination of the contemporary Mexican art scene in *Idols Behind Altars*. Brenner excavates the symbols used by the muralists, which, she explained, retained the marks of history and legend. Hart was urged by friends, Lesley Simpson, a Latin Americanist specialising in cultural history, and, I suspect, O'Malley, to counter his naive view of Mexico. Lesley gave Hart a 'long reading list', and his letters show an increasing deference to anthropologists and historians as he travelled outside the city. 'The more I see the more I realise how intricate the subject is', Hart wrote late in 1931.

At the centre of Hart's poem is the Aztec legend on which Mexico City was built, first called Tenochtitlan. The Nahuatl name Tenochtitlan can be translated as 'among the prickly pears growing in the rocks'. The place was founded in 1325 when, as legend has it, the god Huitzilopochtli directed his nomadic people to settle. They would find an eagle, its talons gripping a nopal growing out of a rock in a lake, a snake in its beak. This sacred spot was where the city must be built.

The nopal is a symbol of resistance in the poem. It seems likely that the ideas that underpin it were developed through his conversations with O'Malley. As a symbol of Mexico, the very boundaries of the plant are 'edge stabbed and pricked', its flesh ripped, gesturing to ongoing tensions along the United States–Mexico border. During the Depression between 1929 and 1936, the United States deported Mexican Americans on an industrial scale. In 1931 a newspaper reported that a single state, California, had deported 70,000 Mexicans. In June, the *Daily Ardmoreite* in Oklahoma reported that 'Officer Kills Two Mexican Youths'. One of the victims was the nephew of the President, Salvador Cortés Rubio.

O'Malley was impatient with the 'usual type of wealthy person who goes out [. . .] to escape humanity or to become interested in ceremonies, dance or legend of the Indians and who does not care a damn for the actual spoliation of Indians or Mexicans there.' These complaints ring true of *The Bridge*, where Hart takes Pocahontas as his own, making her a character in the poem. While she is a clear victim of the settlers' expansion west ('grieving', she mourns 'her chieftain lover'), she is presented as an unreconstructed mother-earth figure, for whom 'a birch kneels', and around whom oaks 'circle in a crash of leaves'. We find her lost in dance as she conjures the risen 'shade' of her lover, with his 'spear and assemblies . . . yelling battlements'.

In 'Nopal', however, the American poet's gaze is met with 'desert disregard', which registers the influence the Irish Republican had on Hart's increasing scepticism of 'induced foreign culture'. In another Mexico fragment, 'The Circumstance', Hart presents a version of himself as 'a bloody foreign clown'. Hart admired the muralist Siqueiros because he felt he was 'most Mexican and himself. The very soil of Mexico seems spread on his canvasses.'

The endless regress of the image of the nopal, as the eyes move over a vast landscape, borrows from the visual language of the muralists, with densely packed crowds seen in Rivera's murals at the Palacio Nacional, for instance, drawing the gaze through dozens of faces out to the ends of the composition. O'Malley's voice, talking Hart through composition and technique, can be heard here. As O'Malley put it in a broadcast, these murals were designed so that 'Line was broken at every possible angle to form recessions'.

O'Malley kept Hart's letters. One had a scribble on the back in Hart's hand: 'Cortez: the Enactment – and he put The Cross upon that people', suggesting the cross was to be a counter image to the nopal in the new poem. In an interview with *El Universal* shortly after his arrival, Hart explained that the poem would be comprised of 'song patterns', 'symphonic voices' that would combine to create a vision of the 'physiognomy of the Mexican landscape'. Looking at the fragments he left behind, it seems that, like the Brooklyn Bridge in his other long poem, the image of the nopal was to be the image around which his new work would revolve – the central phrase of the fugue to be adapted, counterpointed, returned to.

Early in July, Hart was forced to leave his new friend and return to Ohio for his father's funeral. It seems likely that it was at this moment of parting that Hart gave O'Malley the poem. He also offered O'Malley the use of the Mixcoac house while he was away, briefly relieving him of financial pressures before he would drive back to Taos. The two friends would not meet again.

O'Malley knew that there were dangers in stories, the way that they can crystallise around a person or an event. He was troubled by those that were told about Hart. 'I did not like some of the articles that appeared after his death', he wrote, 'and I meant to write of him as I had known him, but I did not.' A good ninety years later, I wanted to finish that project and belatedly correct these articles, sifting through the remnants of conversations, letters, and documents.

I folded over my page and put the book back into my bag. Even with the miraculous heat of the golden bench, I began to get cold. In Uppsala, the buildings were the colours of ice cream. Over the river, snow was heaped in greying piles against pink walls. White blended the blush into the sky, covering a tower that rose behind an arching roof and curved dormer windows. It was beautiful, but I missed our sodden, wooded square in Ireland – particularly after reading O'Malley's painterly writing. Home was, and is, a rented four-room Gate Lodge balanced on the lace-like edges of the border between the counties of Meath and Kildare. Built in the mid-nineteenth century, its ramshackle grey stone and duck-egg blue door mark the entrance to an old Anglo-Irish estate, circled by woodland and ribboned on one side by a narrow stream, and with an Ordnance Survey marker plugged into our garden wall. By June, the waterlogged verges are bright with irises. So many, open-mouthed, that they form a golden haze, the breath of their pollen rising with heat from the afternoon sun.

Such a house exhales and sweats. Its lungs are the central chimney that warms the adjoining rooms through a shared wall. Without the fire lit, the leadlight windows collect water at their points and a layer of moisture slicks the slate floor. I cursed both of these things incessantly before I left, throwing the wet rags used to soak up the mess of the windows into the laundry basket every morning – laundry that, once washed, will not dry.

The Gate Lodge sits between layers of stories, like leaves and matter they fall, rot, and work their way into the soil – what Eavan Boland calls 'sweet corrosion'. Karl and I walk through the gates one morning and find a car stopped outside. The driver leans out and greets us. The dog tugs on the lead, barking at the stranger. The driver tells us that he had great craic in our house, about thirty years ago. He was friends with the chef who lived there when the Big House was still a hotel. One New Year's Eve, they brought in a donkey off the avenue and turned it around in the kitchen – it was a laugh, he said, grinning out of the car window, a bit of good luck.

Down the road at Rodanstown a ring fort rises behind a ruined chapel where glass Coke bottles and beads circle a black-and-white photograph of a priest. It is said that the church is presided over by St Ruadhán of Lorrha, one of the Twelve Apostles of Ireland who were students with St Finnian at Clonard, a monastery deeper west into Meath. We live in the Pale: an area in eastern Ireland under direct rule by the English crown in the late Middle Ages. A hollowed-out tower bound with ivy is what remains of Sir George Wentworth, a Protestant, and his 487 acres. In 1640, the man had 'a large stone house, a Mill, a pigeon house and two farme houses'. Even after his death, Wentworth still provides a dwelling for the area's fat wood pigeons: they arrange each other's lilac and grey feathers, strutting pompously around the rim of the building, singing the same five notes reedy and low. Behind the ruin, fantastic-ally expensive racehorses nibble at the grass, their names printed in gold on their bridles: Irresistible Jewel, Kyprios, Beau Soleil. The hunt appears once a year. Dozens of hounds gather at the gates to the Big House. The dogs swirl around the lamp posts, waiting to tear apart the foxes that we hear at night. Our road is littered with vodka bottles and cans chucked from cars. The sign at the end of it reads: *Maynooth/Maigh Nuad*, meaning 'plain of Nuadha', the first King of the Tuatha Dé Danann, a mythical tribe of the gods. Names that, as Hart put it, are made to 'shift, subvert / And anagrammatize' in the language of a 'stranger tongue' from some absent 'Captain of this doubloon isle', or 'Commissioner of mildew'.

I pulled at the fingers of my gloves, then put my palms down, slotting them under my thighs and lacing my hands together, feeling the warmth of the golden bench reach through the material. The reclined man was like one of Blake's angels, I thought, or perhaps his Milton, muscled and bathed gold. 'Bring me my bow of burning gold! / Bring me my arrows of desire!', writes Blake. I am embarrassed by this poem, what we call 'Jerusalem', but what is actually Blake's preface to *Milton: A Poem in Two Books*. Now, the poem is sung jingoistically, patriotically. But it has been co-opted. It was written as acerbic criticism of rapid industrialisation and the conformist doctrine of the Church of England; the poem leverages a socialist future by conjuring an England that never existed, weaponising nostalgia into something with forward motion. It is a rebel song, which the socialists and suffragists of the early twentieth century knew, singing a version set to music by Hubert Parry.

Still, and despite my love of Blake, I bristle at the lines that pop into my head, but more at the associations that have formed around them than the words themselves. But there is cowardice in that type of embarrassment. There is a type of Englishness that is defined by its own disavowal. I wonder if I fall into this category: extremely English by virtue of my embarrassment at being English. It strikes me as weak thinking that claims ethical superiority to jingoism and nationalism while remaining inert, even nihilistic.

Dreaming of our home and, in doing so, romanticising Ireland, I am flirting with this long and ethically hollow tradition of Englishness. I think of Graham Greene and his lover Catherine Walston on Achill Island in the late 1940s, introduced to the island by O'Malley. They rented a stone cottage in Dooagh, without electricity or tap water, and played at being contented lovers a while. They were both married, though not to each other. Greene wrote novels about their romance. They must have fought with the fire, strung up their laundry in the wet air, the scent of peat swirling from the chimney. I think of a type of English public intellectual who loudly declares that they will pursue an Irish passport through a distant relative. They repeatedly threaten to move to Dublin, or to the striking landscapes of the west coast, where housing is now unafford-able for those born there, threatening the Gaeltacht. England is your country. It is your mess, I want to say, both to them and to myself. I am torn between places. I am ignoring Swedish while taking Irish lessons online and flailing hopelessly with pronun-ciation. I need to unlearn (as my teacher put it) my instinct to come to the sounds of Irish from an English perspective. A Swedish colleague explained to me that we filter out linguistic sounds that we don't use from a very early age; we simply stop hearing them. I turn on Raidió na Gaeltachta and understand nothing.

There was a noise – an odd *clack clack* on stone through wedges of snow. A man in his eighties had sat down on the bench, choosing a spot around the kneecaps. The *clack clack* had come from his crutches, which cut into his thick coat at the elbows. He grinned at me and in that gesture destroyed the narratives I had constructed for Sweden. He began to sing, gesturing at a lamp just turned on in a window across the river:

> Vintern rasat ut bland våra fjällar
> Drivans blommor smälta ner och dö
> Himlen ler i vårens ljusa kvällar
> Solen kysser liv i skog och sjö

Turning towards him, I smiled back. And he nodded, invit-ingly, perhaps expecting me to join in. 'I don't understand, I'm so sorry,' I said. 'English?' I nodded. 'It's a song for spring. Winter rages on the mountain, and the flowers die, of course. But later, the sun will smile on spring's bright evenings, and they will be brought back to life.' 'It's beautiful,' I said. 'Yes,' he said, 'and it won't be long.'

8

A Wedding

Clarence Arthur Crane and his cousin, Orsa Beardsley, set about brushing the horses. They worked until their coats shone, the horses flicking their reddish heads in irritation, impatient for breakfast. The cousins lifted each foot in turn, pulling out the odd stone and bits of muck with small picks. Clarence produced a cloth bag stuffed with tiny flags and scraps of fabric to add to the horses' braids and livery. Orsa rolled his eyes; his cousin could be fussily elaborate. He reached into the bag for a long strip of reds, pinks, greens, and yellows – scraps from the family's general store, which served the centre of a small town in Ohio: Garrettsville.

When the wind was blowing in the right direction across Eagle Creek, Clarence's father's maple syrup cannery washed the town with a malty fragrance. Sometimes the scent crept into train carriages, announcing the stop before the guard had a chance to open his mouth. Today was one of those days, the nose sweetly confusing the tongue. Clarence's Uncle Fred worked at the family store. Fred was a poet, writing reviews for the local paper under a pseudonym. He wrote a thick book and published it himself. Fred liked to wrongfoot newcomers to the store, offering them incomprehensible serpentine explanations when all they wanted was a jar of his brother Arthur's maple syrup.

Clarence had spent days planning the picnic. He was famous for parties, a show-off with a fondness for amateur dramatics. He liked to hide in the drawing-room curtains and recite portions of *Hamlet*, a floating head wrapped in red mugging the famous soliloquy. He pulled his trousers up to his nipples, slouched backwards and, walking crabwise, pushed his bottom jaw as far forward as he could and did his Mark Antony: 'lend me your ears', he might have shouted, his eyes moving side to side as if on a pendulum, prattling about honour and ambition.

Unlike his siblings, Clarence was deeply unmusical. Alice, a little younger, was a fine pianist (later, she would study music and composition), and Bess, the youngest (his favourite), was competent with her violin. Their father Arthur, general merchant and maple syrup canner, played the flute prettily, the 'Birdcatcher's Song' filling the large, wooden house as Alice accompanied him on piano, pausing and chivvying her father along with careful nods. In theory, Clarence played the cornet. The sounds he produced were terrible: honks that had the remarkable ability to sit between three notes at once.

Born in Garrettsville, Ohio, on 5 April 1875, Clarence attended the village schools as a boy. For a time, he studied at Allegheny, a liberal arts college in Pennsylvania. He joined the Phi Gamma Delta fraternity, where he met a dear friend, Newton Byron Madden. In 1894, after two years, Clarence dropped out, unable to see the value in his education. He felt he needed practical training and found a job at the National Biscuit Company in Akron. He travelled, selling sugar wafers, oysterettes and saltines wholesale. He learned strategies: how to identify a product that fulfilled an unknown need, how to scale it up, how to cut costs, swapping quality for widespread availability. Now he was back at the cannery, and he would modernise the business, or else he would strike out on his own.

Clarence and Orsa had borrowed the cart from the store. It was emblazoned on both sides 'Crane Brothers Co.', written in a swirling white hand. Clarence filled two feedbags with oats, topping them with a handful of hay. He wrapped four glasses in a blanket and stashed the lot in the cart, next to a basket of sandwiches and a bottle of lemonade.

They stopped the cart outside a generous house and jumped down into the street in suits the colour of limestone. Clarence waited with the horses while Orsa went to knock. Another pair of cousins eventually emerged: Grace Hart and Jessie Sykes. Clarence glanced over, nodding at Jessie, his date, making her way from the house. His eyes moved to Grace. She was already watching him, one hand wrapped in the bridle, the other curling around the horse's temple, idly scratching an ear, which swivelled to and fro as the animal caught wind of greetings and footsteps.

'We've sandwiches,' he heard Orsa tell Grace, offering an arm, 'and Clarence made lemonade, though it won't be cool by the time we're out there.' She was in front of him. It was rude of him not to come to the door, for the two men not to sit for a moment while she and Jessie got ready. Clarence, puffily handsome, bowed slightly. Grace kept her hands clasped together at her chest. He was Clarence for now, taking a new name, 'C.A.', later on in his career.

Born in 1876, Grace Edna was the youngest of three children born to Clinton Orestes Hart and Elizabeth Belden Hart in Chicago. She was the only child to survive her parents. Her youngest brother, Harry, died of scarlet fever at the age of ten the year she was born. Her second brother, Frank, died at twenty-three in 1893 from a morphine overdose, leaving behind his widow, Zell. This was not talked about.

Grace was tall and fair-haired. She sang (a soprano) and was a fixture of the Chicago society columns. She was excitable and often unwell. She loved cars, and enjoyed driving through the countryside, ruining her hair.

Grace and Jessie both wore white blouses tucked into heavy skirts with broad fantails that kicked out fabric behind them as they walked: lilac for Jessie and navy for Grace. Like the two men, their silhouettes were finished with straw hats, but the brims were so wide that any motions of the head were limited to tiny arcs. Grace found this strategic. The enormous hat hid the full variety of her facial expressions and forced the two men into a deferential angle as they spoke, bending forwards to look up into the straw expanse as they continued with their politely dull questions. On the ride home, Jessie threw back her head laughing at a muttered comment from Grace, the hat found her back and tumbled out of the cart and into the road. Grace mugged at Jessie, half closing her eyes and pulling at the thin scarf she had tied from crown to chin. As children they had played stupid and violent games when they were bored, holding each other's noses as hard as they could. They would sit, arms crossed over, squeezing their thumbs and forefingers against the flesh, staring straight ahead. Whoever let go first lost. One afternoon, Jessie suffered a nosebleed, blood pouring from her lips onto her blouse. Grace looked at her in horror. 'Please don't tell anyone,' she said. Jessie promised, squeezed her hand and poked her cousin hard in the ribs.

At twenty-three, Clarence was stocky and prematurely balding. That afternoon it grew warm; he removed his clothing in increments: jacket, tie, waistcoat buttons, rolled sleeves, waistcoat. Grace, twenty-two, noticed the bright-blue braces at either side of his torso and his broad, tanned forearms. He knew a little about Grace from the town's whispers. He had heard a great deal about her beauty (though, presented with her, he thought it had been minimised by his aunts). And her family: jewellers and California pioneers, old English families that made a great deal of money from gold. Her parents were teachers, of that he was sure; her father had his ears blown out during the Civil War, leading him to the classroom where he met his wife. An uncle was in steel, someone had said.

The Cranes could trace their family back to the *Planter*, which sailed out from England in 1646. They took land in Ohio in Portage County, which was named after an eight-mile path between the Cuyahoga and Tuscarawas rivers established by Native Americans and now sunk beneath Akron. Among the milling ghosts of Cranes, Streators and Beardsleys, are revolutionary soldiers, a relative of John Adams, a state legislator who submitted his reports in verse, and one Rollin Crane who took twenty-five men past streaking Confederate bullets as they journeyed down the Mississippi river to seize the town of Vicksburg, just to the west of Jackson. Born in 1820, Sylvina Streator taught herself to read, became a teacher and married

Arthur's father, Edward Manly Crane. Sylvina died in 1914 at the age of ninety-three, living to see her great-grandson, Hart, into his teenage years.

In 1870, Arthur Crane married Ella Melina Beardsley. Their first child, Verdi, was born the following year. She died at the age of ten when Clarence was six, her name passed on, slightly changed, to her youngest sister, Elizabeth (Bess) Verde. Clarence's father was restless, running a variety of businesses. He had the cannery, the family's general store, and directed the local National Bank. Arthur would outlive both his son and grandson, dying in 1939 and leaving behind piles of family records and his own poems.

A story was emerging: by the afternoon, Clarence's affections had transferred from Jessie to this bracing young woman, Grace. In the days after the picnic, the story took shape. Clarence, in love, wrote dozens of letters to her. In the late spring of 1898 he followed her to Chicago. He took with him chocolates and flowers. She said no until she said yes, yes I will.

That June the wealthy brides of Chicago wore white satin and bodices of liberty silk. Their dresses were trimmed with Brussels lace, ribbons girding their fanciful structures. Their heads were shielded with tulle veils and orange blossoms. They carried papery bundles of sweet peas, and breakfasted in family apartments.

On the evening of 1 June, Grace waited for her new husband. She closed one eye a fraction as she checked the placement of the colour on her lips and watched herself in a hotel mirror, dusting her face and breasts with powder. The rose-scented grains fell, grazing the light fabric of her nightdress.

The day's piles of silks and linen were washed, folded, stored away in cabinets, ready to be used for the first bed of another pair of young lovers, or scrunched into the bride's trousseau. The wispy fabric that had first concealed and revealed Grace's body stayed among her belongings. Passed down and passed down until it found itself labelled in a brown carton in Ohio: 'Box 6: A Nightgown worn by Grace Hart Crane, poet's mother, on her wedding night.'

The couple returned to Garrettsville. Clarence worked at his father's syrup cannery. Arthur built a house, linked to his own by a garden, as a wedding present for Clarence and Grace. Within two years, there were curtains of ivy drawn around the porch. A little over a year after the marriage, Hart made his way. Harold Hart Crane was born at 1068 Freedom Street on 21 July 1899. Hart liked to say that he was born with a 'little toenail in the last century'. It was relatively cool for Ohio in high summer, just touching thirty degrees. Still, it was hot. And hotter still to be in labour. It must have been stifling that day, adding to the difficulties of breathing hard during the birth in a hot wooden room. She panted the baby out, her inhalations sharp in her chest, so sure that he, like his father, would be asthmatic and would struggle to breathe in the heat and the close air.

He was a sweet and strange boy. He spoke, read and walked early, developing an advanced vocabulary and a surreal sense of humour. He loved the garden between the houses. He enjoyed sitting at the piano in his grandmother's parlour, teasing out melodies by ear. He learned with his aunt Alice. She found his lack of consistency and nervousness frustrating. He told her that he was too nervous to practise, or to learn the principles of complex harmonies. 'But he never really finished anything. He was far too impatient', she said. He preferred playing things like ' "Marche Grotesque." He would play it over and over, each time a little louder.'

At times Hart seemed oddly literal, telling his father that he couldn't sleep because he hadn't yawned. He loved his mother's hats. He spent hours alone in the house raking through her drawers for ribbons, feathers and buttons to stitch onto them, until his Aunt Bess intervened – by then Bess Madden, married to Clarence's best friend. Aunt Bess took the beautiful, textured materials away, suggesting he play with toy soldiers or lead animals instead. He cried for days. One afternoon, he walked into the town's ice-cream parlour and scanned the rows and rows of bright-coloured, impossible-seeming flavours and asked for a codfish soda. There is a particular way that a child can at once register their suspicion, testing the adult in question, while all the time forcefully hoping they can do anything. In this case, to magic any possible flavour or combination with a flourish of the ice-cream scoop, diving into the generously filled stainless steel.

9

Mixcoac Flower Garden

It was 1 May 1931, a Friday. Hart stood outside his new home in Mixcoac. It was the first house he had ever rented; the first property he had signed for in years. Before him was an old, flat-roofed house comprised of eight rooms. Geometric ironwork bound the curved and gently corniced windows at its front. For fifty dollars a month Hart could rent the house and retain two servants to cook, clean and help him with the garden. Hart had to 'squirm' for the money to take it, borrowing from his father, but he was convinced a house of his own would have 'creative advantages'. He wrote to friends in New York, explaining the relief he felt in 'having a place of my own – really for the first time in my life'.

A flower garden skirted three sides of the house. It had violets, irises, nasturtiums, calla lilies, freesias, roses, calendulas, cannas, pansies, feverfew, candytuft, morning glories, a rhododendron bush that had been steadily batted back to the perimeters. Tuberoses, a favourite, scented the air. Their perfume grew heavier as the evening approached, and hundreds of white, trumpet-shaped blooms slowly opened, reaching out to greet the night.

Hart had the DTs. In the past, he had seen rats clawing at seawater, the rat-poodle pacing around the bars of La Santé in Paris. With the distortions of his illness, combined with his perpetual hay fever, the colourful scene as he looked at the house, with the heat and the altitude, might have been discomforting, warped by his sense that he couldn't possibly deserve it, he who had abused Porter at her gate, who had so embarrassed the Foundation, who had taken advantage of Zinsser's generosity.

Hart's anxiety brought with it an exaggerated awareness of sounds and smells. The smallest noise could cause a lasting disruption, which he felt as vibrations in the body long after it had passed. Pleasant smells could induce gagging. Hart's descriptions of the way that loud sounds seemed to lodge in his flesh made sense to me. The body has its own way of remembering. I still start violently with sudden noises. The flashes in my peripheral vision can be unsettling: magical shapes that disappear or change in size with a second look. When I am tired, my senses become untrustworthy. I smell and see things that are not there. Neutral things are suddenly repulsive: fresh tap water smells stagnant. The steam that rises from the dishwasher makes me gag. I wonder if it smells like the scent of a subway grate, or sweat, or water lying on a manhole cover, or pooled at the edge of a kerb, where my head might have laid before I was lifted into the ambulance.

I see him gasping a little with the altitude, the sun, then, uncomfortably hot, high over a confusion of gently swaying smudges and patterns, with single blades of grass that lurched into focus with each step against a vague wash of green. The mixing scents of the roses and lilies might distort, becoming a bottle of perfume dropped in a packed train carriage that mingles with sweat and dog shit clinging to a shoe. Or an embrace: a friend grown inured to their cologne, the splashes growing more liberal with each passing year. Dabs behind the ears, and pressing the wet remainder along the hem of a skirt so that the nauseous scent wakes with every movement. Add to it a cockerel: black-and-orange feathers that rustle as the bird struts over to appraise the intruder, registering the affront with a squawk and a spring of the shoulders. Something that nuzzled. A big head pressed into the back of a knee. A goat wanting at his trousers. And finally, thank God, what looked like a snow fox but, on closer inspection, was a spitz, waiting on the steps with its tail raised and bent like a question mark.

Unfurnished, the house made its own most pure and bare music. He needed to buy every 'nail, griddle, bowl and pillow', filling the rooms with finds from nearby markets and his travels outside the city. First, the indispensables: a broom, a tea kettle, mop, mattress. Then to stuff the frame: hand-carved and lacquered trays, crockery, serapes, toys, hats, Guadalajara pottery, embroideries. And armfuls of flowers from his own garden. The bells of San Juan Evangelista and Santa Maria de Guadalupe rang out once, twice, three times. Hart heard them. Porter heard them. Octavio Paz heard them and roused himself. Hart took out his typewriter, planning another, longer letter of apology for Porter.

Hart had written to her once already, just a brief note as he had emerged from the terror of the past week ('novelty and turmoil', he wrote a month later). This most recent episode had lasted six days, the last few funded by Zinsser's tab at the Mancera. Humiliation, drink, humiliation – it went on. He came out of it suddenly. On Thursday, something in this machinery dislodged just enough to break the cycle. Hart got to work, warding off the inevitable, lowering cloud of shame with practical concerns and attempts to correct his appalling behaviour. He began a new round of apologies, writing first to contacts at the Guggenheim. 'This is as near as I dare come to you today', Hart told Porter in a handwritten note, 'shame and chagrin overwhelm me. I hope you can sometime forgive'. She did, though not in perpetuity. 'The recent cyclone is my last – at least for a year', he said. Hart's jaunty apologies were increasingly insufficient, weighed against the barrages of drunken insults. 'I have no clear recollection of everything said during those times', Hart admitted a few months later, 'but I must have been pretty awful.'

Porter's forgiveness had its limits; Hart would need to find his own accommodation after leaving the hotel. Living together had been disastrous, drawing out their most destructive and malign instincts. Moisés Sáenz had stepped in to find Hart somewhere to live. Within hours he had secured this house. Sáenz was concerned; he cared enough for Hart to try to prise him out of his most recent relapse, perhaps to inspire him back into writing. Both, the teacher surmised, might be achieved with an immediate trip out to his ranch in Taxco. It was decided: he would collect Hart on Saturday, before he had too much time to sit and stew in the empty house. He felt 'jittery', Hart told Porter. He was anxious and shaking. He was off the drink, he assured her, with one full day under his belt, almost two. It was a daily practice. It was hard, foolish even, to promise more.

Sáenz's instinct that a brief trip out to the countryside might soothe Hart was correct. Hart loved to be outdoors, learning about Mexican culture beyond the city. He took photographs, capturing the twin bell towers of the cathedral. After his return to Mixcoac, he continued, immersing himself in the garden outside and neglecting his correspondence. He preferred to 'fuss around' with the flowers. In June, the house was a little louder. Hart's servants, Daniel Hernandez, who was Indigenous Mexican, and his wife, her name has been lost, moved in with their two children. Hart paid them $8 a month. They developed a friendship of sorts, drinking together. Late in the year, Daniel and Hart took a cab out to the Basílica Menor de Nuestra Señora de Guadalupe in Pachuca de Soto, Hidalgo, on her feast day. Hart took his camera, capturing images of the church, cloaked musicians, and women seated and preparing food. Daniel restrained Hart from photographing the day's religious rituals – a spiritual transgression.

Hart loved his first family home, with its generous garden. When he was tiny, he followed Arthur Crane around the paths. They stopped by a vine and Hart pointed to the grapes and said: 'Grandfather, when are you going to pick your peas?' He spent a great deal of time in his grandparents' house, looking at the same view from the opposite direction. In Mixcoac, he had his own version of the Garrettsville house, realising, as he told a friend, a 'long suppressed passion for a few plants and a philosopher's walk'.

In letters between his mother and hers, his grandmother Elizabeth Hart, the three share careful descriptions of prized bouquets. Elizabeth sketched out her sunroom for her grandson: roses in twelve colours, their 'half blown' and blousy heads tilting off their stems. A dozen white peonies beside, most perfect when, half billowing, the flower seems to resist its own bloom.

In a poem, the single image of 'one floating flower' could be made, he knew, to contain 'sleep, death, desire'. Hart loved 'tree names, flower names', the 'ritual of sap and leaves', the 'crash of leaves'. Still lifes found their way into his writing. In 'Sunday Morning Apples', he addressed the Cleveland painter William Sommer in the moment of arranging a new composition:

> Put them again beside a pitcher with a knife,
> And poise them full and ready for explosion –
> The apples, Bill, the apples!

In the painting, Sommer places a bright-blue jug in the centre of a window. A single stem droops from its side, with three vermilion apples scattered at the base. He includes the untouched white pages of his sketchbook at the bottom of the frame. Just as Hart has it in the poem, the painting suspends Sommer in beginning, the act of preparing the scene before he started work.

As it was for Eve and for the artists that have followed her, for Hart gardens represented intellectual, erotic and artistic cravings (unconstrained, and in all combinations). 'The apple on its bough is her desire', wrote the twenty-one-year-old Hart in 'Garden Abstract'. Hart means both that Eve simply wants to take the fruit – that she desires it – but also that the apple symbolises desire itself, abstract and removed from its objects; it *is* her desire. Knowing what you want requires a knowledge of what it is to want and what it is to lack. When Eve tastes the apple, she experiences both at the same time: painful and euphoric knowledge.

Like the young poet trying to assert his developing voice, Eve, knowledge seeker, is set on a path to seize her own cravings and ambitions. 'And so she comes to dream herself the tree', Hart continues in 'Garden Abstract'. Eve comes to dream that she might be a source of knowledge, to be creative in some way.

Grace wrote poems in the guise of her son. I, at nineteen, channelled a frenetic energy into parsing and collecting his poems. I sat among friends while my lover read to them: poems that figured my mental illness as a homunculus, a foul creature tapping against the glass while we slept. I remember them as being good poems. It is true that I was difficult. I threw tantrums and cried constantly, I saw visions and demanded immediate rescuing, utterly panicked. I was an emotional coward. I loved him completely – he first handed me the purple book of Hart's. We were both young. My friends clapped for the poems. I wanted to soar suchwise.

Around the time Hart was writing his poem to Sommer, he was helping his friends William Slater and Susan Jenkins Brown to renovate a farmhouse in Dutchess County, New York. The property, which they called Robber Rocks, looked up into the Catskills, and was sat on a large patch of land where the Browns could establish a smallholding. There was land enough for vegetable patches, orchards, and fruit bushes. Thinking of his grandfather, perhaps, Hart noted the sap maples in his letters.

Hart planted peas and beans and tended to 'a whole menu of delicious vegetables'. There were a dozen or so quince trees with pale-gold and soft-skinned fruit that reminded him of hands slipped into kid gloves, with fingers drawn together into a purse that lifts into the sky. Hart worked through large plots of bushes, picking huckleberries, elderberries, cloudy-blue blueberries, shiny currants, and sour gooseberries with short tails that needed to be shucked.

He slept well there. His physical health started to improve. He enjoyed the silence, 'a quietness that is a tonic after the endless noise and reverberation of New York'. He felt the vibrations even in his sleep, he wrote. Susan felt that Hart drank 'for its release of tension'. It induced behaviour that 'he could not bear to recall'. Staying with the Browns, Hart swore off Bill's applejack and homemade ale, fermenting in a crock pot and sped along by the warmth of the chimney. The ongoing, debilitating bladder infections, headaches, insomnia, and gastric problems were relieved, Hart claimed, through a combination of abstinence from alcohol, calm surroundings, vigorous exercise and a diet of fresh vegetables, eggs and butter and milk from a nearby farm with cream so thick that you could push the disc of it with your thumb, down into the neck where it would melt into the liquid.

When I arrived back in Ireland in the first days of summer in 2022, I found comfort in the cottage and garden: a square carved out of the woods. I had left Sweden shortly after my conversation with the elderly man on the golden bench. The sand was dissolving, structures collapsing in on themselves. I was exhausted and growing paranoid, figures were flickering in the corners of my eyes, or looming over me while I slept. I had a pervasive sense that I had done something horribly wrong. I would be found out and punished. When I ate, tastes changed suddenly, becoming disgusting. My hair was falling out, chunks of it sticking to my fingers in the shower. My diary from the period is confusing. It contains a mixture of descriptions of pulls from a pack of Tarot cards, which I began using because the invented futures my imagination was conjuring were torturous – it was healthier to believe the cards. There were near-daily admissions that 'I feel low', then 'I am retreating'. I stopped contacting my friends. Those that were around me were cruelly reduced in spidery handwriting, becoming 'untrustworthy cunts', 'manipulators', 'overbearing'. I was still trying to write, but all that would emerge from hours of staring were short chunks, the briefest of vignettes without any through line or connecting thoughts. I could not make it cohere. I packed and cleaned my room. In the taxi on the way to the airport, my mind collapsed: my hands shook. I couldn't breathe and I retched, convinced that I was about to die.

It was unnaturally hot in Ireland that summer. The house was drying out, paint cracking around the window frames. I passed Hart's final age. I dug up the vegetable patch and planted it with seedlings, the radish stems quickly trimmed by rabbits, the autumn broccoli trampled by escaped sheep. I stripped and painted furniture, waiting for my thoughts to reform. Waiting for it to dry, I sat with the dog on the front step, listening to the rooks in the yew. One is an excellent mimic, able to approximate the cadence of my voice.

Years later, Hart's friends remembered him ferrying logs back and forth from the store to the fire. He goofed and laughed so infectiously that the Browns' young son, Gwiffy, would be swept into irrepressible giggles. If something struck Hart as particularly hilarious, he would repeatedly slap his own thigh. He was energetic and, according to his mother, 'either up or down, he was always vital, and held your interest and sympathy.' He was a gossip. He loved animals, calling the 'famished kitten' who stars in his poem 'Chaplinesque' Agrippina and then, on discovering she was a he, 'Agrippenis'. Bill Wright remembered him as cheerful. The last time he saw him was in August 1931. Bill caught a glimpse of Hart on a bus heading out to Lake Erie, passing by his house. He was sat near the back, reading a book.

Susan Jenkins Brown declared her frustration with the temptation of his friends to stress his 'darker aspect' to his biographers. She urged readers to go to his letters to get the true measure of him. She acknowledges his 'nerves', and difficulty managing the demands of employers, his lower moods, and the increasing chokehold of his depressions, but emphasises his gentleness and spontaneity. He was boyish, his friend Waldo Frank said, always 'looking around obviously for something to love. Something great.' There was 'something spring-like about him'. After long dinners, Hart stood at the sink for hours, washing dishes for the family and the guests that tumbled in and out – poets and writers bracing themselves for a walk home through thick snow under a cloak of bootlegged cider and raisin wine.

'This is the kind of place I am going to have when I can afford it', he told Grace and Elizabeth, in a letter written from the Browns'. The house in Mexico offered him a glimpse of that place of his own, if only for a year. He tried to settle. Still agitated he sat down to write another note of apology to Porter. His hands shook. 'When I next get D.T.'s again I'll just take it out on police', he wrote, referring to his outburst at her gate. 'They'll at least have a cell for me – or a straitjacket', he added.

Like his poem to Bill, and Bill's own painting, Hart was suspended, caught in the space between the idea for his new poem and its execution. Though the poem remained unfinished, and exists only as a collection of ideas, Hart seems to have found its tentative beginnings outdoors in the language of plants and flowers.

10

Life Saver Candies

C.A.'s most significant achievement was the invention of the Life Saver candy. This round, punctured sweet – known to me as a child in England as a Polo mint – was intended as a summer treat, a hard candy that, unlike C.A.'s chocolates, would be resilient in the hot Ohio summers, even when jammed into a pocket in their paper tube. C.A. had the idea after setting up his own business, the Crane Chocolate Co., established in April 1911.

C.A. named the sweets 'Life Savers' because, once cut, they resembled lifebuoys. I thought this as a child, looking at the sticky mints in my hands and the rings that lined the beaches that edged the town where I was born.

Bexhill-on-Sea has the particular faded glamour of the Victorian seaside resort: intricately constructed terraces with domed roofs; old, two-star hotels fronted with steps up to stuffy pink or sage-green upholstered receptions; rows and rows of beach huts with women on stools sat just inside the doors, reading or listening to the radio. A long promenade dotted with the flashing lights of arcades and music pavilions painted white with red accents, cafes where you could buy egg and chips and a cup of tea for – back then – a couple of pounds. In the summer there were trucks with ice-cream sellers sinking Flakes deep into the thick, quickly melting cream of a 99 and rollerskating children drawing figures of eight around pensioners making their way along the prom from bench to bench.

My maternal grandmother and I liked to visit the De La Warr Pavilion, a 1935 building designed to look like an ocean liner flanking the shore. Inside, there is a staircase that curves up the insides like a snail's shell. My grandma and I would sit on the long terrace that looked out to the Channel with a hot drink, perhaps with a slice of cake or a cheese scone, roughly split in two and stacked with butter pooling into the dough. In the summer, there might be music played from the bandstand: a white structure that looks like a cross between a clamshell and a handkerchief caught by the wind.

One winter, there was a fierce storm. Mum took my brother and I down to the front. We held her hands and leaned forward, the wind bearing our weight. I looked out at the sea and saw the storm as it was in one of my favourite children's books, with a giant, blue, green- and grey-striped paw followed by whiskers and pointed ears – a cat sweeping through the waves, chasing fishing boats.

We walked on a little, past the Pavilion, and saw a group of men working quickly, hauling dinghies from the stones up onto the tarmac. I spotted him. 'Daddy!' I shouted down, my voice thin in the gale. He grinned and waved up at us in his red drysuit. I have always loved the sea – another reason why I might have loved Hart, the great sea poet, with such fierce immediacy.

> O brilliant kids, frisk with your dog
> Fondle your shells and sticks, bleached
> By time and the elements . . .

At nursery, I was taken to the beach one extremely hot afternoon in August, around my birthday. I had forgotten my bathing suit. Dressed in blue shorts and a T-shirt, I was intent on swimming. I bolted from the teacher and flung myself into the water. I was explosively energetic, occasionally malign. I lit a match and held it outstretched in front of my chest before dropping it down the back of my T-shirt as my mum looked up, all because she was busy with my brother.

In the summer, if I was lucky, I spent the day on Dad's boat. Walking next to the hull in the small waves, I would hop in and perch as Dad pushed from behind, soon leaping in himself, taking the ropes of the mainsail and adjusting until he caught the wind. My job, when we were out far enough, was to work the front sail as we raced around the course. If the wind was strong enough, I would pull out the spinnaker. The purple sheet would billow, and I would copy my dad, adjusting with tiny movements until I felt the wind suddenly tug us forward. Strapped into a harness, I made the most of my negligible weight, leaning out as far as I could, feeling as though I might fall, the salt and wind grazing my cheeks through a thick layer of sun cream. The blue and pink ropes were tight in my gloved hands, as I tried to harness the wind, seeking the best angle for the sail.

I wonder if this memory is the most significant achievement of my relationship with my father. I wonder if it is enough. It is not possible to summarise a complex relationship in an anecdote or statement, even one that is now non-existent, to declare someone a bad father or a bad mother. It would be simplistic to route all problems back to that first troubled relationship.

For all the endless tragedies that litter that degraded bond, there were summers where we sped along, fast as anything and I grinned, or we capsized and I cried, suddenly aware of the endless water under my feet. Dried off and presented with a large glass of Coke and a bowl of steaming chips in the bar, I remember declaring: 'Daddy, you look like a Battenberg cake,' pointing at the distinct, outrageous stripes on his arms, tanned from different wetsuits. 'So do I, though,' I said, proudly looking down at the contrast between my upper arms and forearms.

'You are undoubtedly a Bratton,' my maternal grandmother had said to me when I was about seven, taking in my dark hair, thick eyebrows, mossy eyes, large, upturned nose and olive skin – pale, but quick to tan. I have, like my father, a sharp, triangular chin and a deranged-looking, broad smile. My mum's side is fair, blonde and blue-eyed and extremely prone to sunburn, rounder in the face and with brows in echoing, elegant curves, scooping up and around the eyes. I see him in the mirror when my jaw is set, and when my face breaks into laughter. But my voice is my mother's.

Ernie O'Malley's son, Cormac, has written that, as an adult, he began to build a sense of his father for future biographers, and for his own 'fund of knowledge'. The work was piecemeal, with letters and stories accrued by writing to O'Malley's friends, beginning by asking 'the obvious questions'.

Sat in the National Library of Ireland in Dublin, I wrote these phrases down in my notebook: 'the obvious questions', 'fund of knowledge'. It is odd to realise that you would have no idea what these questions might be in relation to your own father, or to have the information and tools to write even the slightest biography of their life. I could say, vaguely, where he was born, and I could pursue research to sketch out a sense of his career and what his job entailed.

Working in Hart's papers in New York earlier that year, I had been trying to rebuild my sense of his mother, piecing together her movements and relationships. O'Malley's papers, which I saw the same week, were highly unusual. They suggested an immediate impression of the man: there were jammed note-books, recording everything, and lists and lists, gathering together books, artworks, housed within master lists. These taxonomies tried to get a handle on every book read, collected or loaned, every artwork bought, but giving a great sense of loss, of things and ideas slipping through his fingers, uncaptured or unfinished.

That morning I had made my way from our Gate Lodge into Dublin in search of O'Malley's writings on the muralists. It was September 2022. I had averted disaster by spending the majority of the summer watching the garden, but I was still tired. In the space between sleeping and waking I was being visited. I hallucinated grasping figures leaning over the bed. The previous night in the early hours a small boy rested his hand gently on the radiator. He blinked and caught my gaze. I got out of bed, waking as I pulled apart the heavy curtains, looking out into the violent emerald of the yew.

The bus rolled through Celbridge, County Kildare, a tight turn on the river, and I closed my eyes as my stomach lurched. For the briefest moment I was presented with a series of images. In one I stood in our kitchen and took the point of a slim knife from the drawer and pushed it across the golden top of my forearm. In another I was on the bridge below the bus, the grey and fast-flowing water beneath my feet. These intrusive images did not present sincere suggestions. I tried to examine their intrusion with curiosity, as I had been taught. I traced them back to my fleeting desires to be able to observe the pain that springs shoots so quietly, spreads and flowers, because physical things seem more real.

The morning traffic was bad and we waited by the Four Courts. People in suits carrying stacks of files weaved in and out of brownish-grey columns. A square of green was just visible through a series of archways, bisected with iron gates. Built in the late eighteenth century and restored in 1932, the colonial-style neoclassical structures form quadrangles, split and raised by ornate pillars – an arrangement that is both mathematically pleasing and facilitates observation. A Corinthian portico faces the river and a verdigris dome tops a round, internal hall, once populated by sculptures of Irish lawyers and judges in its recesses. Cake-frosting stucco edges the joins between the walls and the curved ceiling.

We turned right and crossed the river, where I hopped off to walk to the National Library. I spent the morning reading O'Malley's essays and reviews. In my chair I was enveloped in dark wood and silence, broken occasionally by the grate of a pencil sharpener or the turning of dusty pages. The library's vast, circular ceiling was painted in rhythmic shades of spearmint. If I could float into the top of the curve, and if I spoke or sang or screamed as I did so, the noise would resound clear and fresh, bouncing off the walls and back into the centre.

I swapped the essays and reviews for a stack of biographies. Leafing through military histories I grew frustrated, struggling to grasp the complex man that Hart knew, and that I had slowly started to see emerge through his letters and in his archives in New York. I gave up. I was chasing a hare, darting in and out of thickets – it was a distraction. I went home and crawled into bed.

The information I have about my own father is experiential and derived from a short period. It is sourced from the impressions of an adoring child: aged three she is tired in the woods and shouts 'Pick up!' until he relents. Proudly, she musses his black hair from above. A four-year-old presses a poster of a stealth bomber to a bedroom wall, her brother glues together a matching Airfix model and places it on the windowsill. On her fifth birthday, she takes out a big, black pen and writes her name across the wrong part of her new, pink satchel, a gift from her dad: FRANCESCA, she prints, in wonky letters, diagonally across the visible flap, and not on the inside as he specified. He was annoyed. 'I love it!' said Mum when I got home, 'it's *your* writing!'

On 1 April a six-year-old is bent double with laughter because she has been tricked into thinking a snake had climbed up into a tree, visible from the house. That autumn she is barrelled into the mud by a golden retriever swerving around a corner. 'You're all right,' he says, picking her up and hoisting her onto his shoulders. He makes sure that she pets the next dog they see on the walk. Seven, perhaps, and the pretty woman in the bakery is handing me and my brother a box of doughnuts. Dad doesn't pay. I say they are too sweet. I lie, telling her that I hate custard and so does my mummy. I am being deliberately cruel when I say this; they divorced when I was eighteen months old, and I have no memory of their marriage.

On New Year's Eve at the sailing-club disco, the doughnut woman is inexplicably there. She walks up to me and tells me that my father is extremely funny. She asks me if he will dance with her. I am so sure that he will say no that I pass on the message. Sat on a tapestry chair at the side of the wood-panelled room, I glimpse them moving together through various sets of legs as the DJ plays 'Last Train to London' and 'Boogie Wonderland'.

The memories start to thin out. A furious teenager asks questions about the planes as they drive to her grandma's. 'He just works on small sections,' he says. 'But as a whole they are designed to kill people,' she says, 'do you ever think about that?' 'Each plane a hurtling javelin', wrote Hart in 'Cape Hatteras', as they launch with the 'razor sheen' of the sun glancing off their fuselage up into 'a screeching gale to hover'. The two planes set each other in their sights. The lucky one pumps lead into the other's shell before it tilts and falls.

I used to wonder if he would appear if I broke my leg, or an arm – something significant. Perhaps if I ran out into traffic, and was entirely covered in plaster, limbs hoisted on various slings. At eighteen I was subjected to real terror – a moment in a night that changed my life. He did not come. I still worry that writing this might hurt him (might hurt *you*, it's not too late).

Hart's poems are shot through with different forms of grief and longing, romantic and platonic. I suspect that I was always drawn to the absences that haunt Hart's poems, the way they try to bridge losses – hands that cannot quite reach each other, gazes that are not met, calls that do not receive a response.

In 'Indiana' a woman, thinking of her absent son, remembers when she and her late husband 'once rode off' from their own parents. They sought their fortune in the studded hills out

West. They 'Waved Seminary Hill a gay good-bye . . . / We found God lavish there in Colorado', she says, recalling how 'golden syllables loosed from the clay'.

Hart originally wrote this poem in the voice of a father. But in the late 1920s he abandoned it. He could not finish it. Eventually he decided to invert the voice, changing it to a mother's call. This seems to reflect the shift in his relationship with his parents late in the 1920s. By May 1928, after his argument with Grace in California, he was estranged from his mother, and was slowly repairing his once fraught relationship with his father.

C.A. loved his son. In 1917 he reassured Hart after Grace's suicide attempt, telling his son that 'you are the only treasure I have on God's green earth'. Hart had felt stuck between his parents from an early age, which crippled his relationship with his father for many years. When the two slowly started to rebuild it, it was in the wake of his break with his mother. It was not possible to hold them both close at once. I hear Grace in the final lines on 'Indiana':

> Come back to Indiana – not too late!
>   (Or will you be a ranger to the end?)
> Good-bye . . . Good-bye . . . oh, I shall always wait
>   You, Larry, traveller –
>   stranger,
>   son,
>   – my friend–

I hear her desperation, what Hart understood as suffocation. The playwright Tennessee Williams heard the same. Entirely drunk, he appeared on television in 1971 and declared his funeral wishes: 'Place my bones close to the bones – the submerged bones – of Hart Crane,' Williams said. 'Hart Crane had a life very similar to mine,' he explained. 'He had a very worldly father. His father was involved in the manufacture of candy. Mine in shoes. And we had very similar backgrounds. He was overly devoted to his mother as I was to mine . . . And we both wrote out of an intense personal need.'

This 'personal need' Williams describes seems to be the impossibility of being close to both parents. After Williams explained his and Hart's shared closeness with their mothers, the interviewer responded: 'Was he also homosexual?' Williams: 'Yes, he was indeed, and he made absolutely no disguise of the fact. And he shocked people a great deal.' The interviewer: 'It must have brought a lot of pain into his life at that point?' Williams: 'Whether it did or not he didn't care. He drank heavily, unfortunately. But I don't think he gave a damn whether he shocked people. And I've never cared whether I shocked people. Because I think people who are shocked by the truth are not deserving of the truth.'

Williams is talking for both writers, bundling their stories together. He reaches for a book of Crane's poems on the table and explains: 'Now this is not one of his poems that is most critically acclaimed, but is one of the most moving ones,' he says, opening the book at 'Indiana'. He read the poem in full, eyes brimming. He bites through the line 'I shall always wait'. In his mouth it is a threat. In *Steps Must Be Gentle*, a one-act play, Williams picked at Grace and Hart's relationship again, imagining Grace crying out to her dead son. 'I wake up calling incessantly in the night,' she tells him, 'How kind of you to finally respond.'

Williams clung on to the idea that his relationship with his mother held the key to his unhappiness. Perhaps he found this idea in a damaging and internalised homophobic cliché, rooted in degraded interpretations of Freud, wherein the male child identifies with the mother, loving 'boys whom he loves in the way in which his mother loved him when he was a child.'

Before he left for Mexico, Hart went to a good friend (and Sam's business partner at their bookshop, Dauber and Pine) Solomon Grunberg for advice. The two would walk block after block in Manhattan, talking. On one occasion, Hart came to Grunberg with an unwholesome dream about Grace. It was physiological. He was searching through Grace's entrails. He was looking for some kind of symbolism in it, Grunberg said.

Hart looked for solace in Grunberg's Freudian models. Grunberg had told him he was a 'Platonist', 'searching like all Platonists for the highest good'. He would not, Grunberg explained, be able to achieve his poetic goals unless he repaired his relationship with his father. The relationship with Grace did not need to be salvaged, he said. Mother and son were too 'horribly involved'. It was a 'chronic situation'. Their relationship was irreparable, Grunberg told John Unterecker, a poet, professor of English at Columbia University and one of Hart's biographers. 'He would always break,' Grunberg explained, 'I never kept a count of how many times they reconciled.' But in Grunberg's world, Hart's relationship with his father was paramount. It was this rupture that, Grunberg said, 'drove him to drink instead of to the writing of poetry'.

The psychoanalyst and writer Adam Phillips tells us that 'biography should be a refuge from the scapegoating of parents.' Narratives of Hart's life that blame his instability and eventual death on his mother's overbearing, narcissistic presence might do well to heed Phillips's advice, and might consider where this reductive model might originate. We might allow his mother the same grace as they do Hart, considering the genuine psychological suffering that resulted in her institutionalisation when Hart was a boy. As Colm Tóibín has written, Hart and Grace seemed to 'share' a particular 'emotional instability'. Another kind of 'dim inheritance', whether environmental or genetic.

His relationship with his mother severed after their arguments in California in 1928, Hart sought out his father. Hart's time at Canary Cottage in Chagrin Falls helped repair their bond. In Mexico City, Hart befriended Hazel Cazes, a past assistant of C.A.'s in his New York office, who was living nearby with her husband. Cazes had worked as a go-between for C.A. and Hart when he was seventeen. Now, aged thirty-one, he sought her out again. She looked after him, as she had when he was a boy, cooking him meals and lending him money. In turn, she sent letters back to C.A. with notes on how Hart was coping, recording his health problems, drinking levels, and spending habits.

C.A.'s letters to Hart in Mexico are kind, not loaded with increasingly weary demands that Hart seek more stable employment, as they were in the previous decade. He was firm, though. When Hart pressed him for cash he reminded his son that he was 'in Mexico to work and study and not to entertain . . .' 'I really don't think you need it', he added, urging Hart to live within the means of the Guggenheim. He knew 'full well' that he would need to support Hart after the award's expiration, needs that he guessed were 'not apparent' to his son just now, so focused was he on daily survival.

Hart's last letter to his father has been lost. C.A.'s response, though, has survived. He told his son that he missed him and instructed Hart to write to him once a week. He recounted a recent visit from his own father, Arthur, and reassured Hart that his feeling that Mexico was losing the sheen of recent arrival was natural; it meant he was beginning to settle in. 'All of us find out that there are certain illusions that we make and later discover that there are strange conditions in our lives', wrote C.A. He hoped Hart would return to him in Chagrin Falls soon, after the end of his Fellowship: 'I am sure you will be glad to come back to the best place on earth', he wrote, 'there are a lot worse men than your old father.'

On 6 July 1931, Bessie sent Hart an urgent telegram; C.A. was very sick. He had suffered a stroke while visiting the Chagrin Falls post-office at 8.30 that morning. He was taken home, where he remained unconscious until his death. His death notice listed his active businesses: Crane Chocolate Co., the Crane Co. (his retail business), Cartier Chocolate Co. (a subsidiary), Canary Cottage and the Academy Bell, a restaurant in Hudson. At one time, C.A. had five retail stores in Cleveland. He was a mason and a member of the Phi Gamma Delta fraternity, the notice records. The notice does not mention Grace, but includes Hart, 'a son by a former marriage ... awarded a $2,500 fellowship for work in creative poetry in Mexico City'.

Bessie urged Hart to come home immediately. But he was paranoid, stuck in a loop where events seemed to unfold to enable his persecution. He momentarily thought it was all a trick, that the Guggenheim Foundation was trying to lure him out of the country, fed up with his erratic behaviour. His drinking had grown worse, with 'pulque sprees three times a day'.

He had been testing the Foundation's patience, after his ejection from a party at the American Embassy a fortnight ago. Hart had planned a dinner with Porter after she had swung by the house. She interrupted Hart. He had been reading Blake, the pages lit with a candle. She lingered at his gate and they spoke about his plans for the garden. 'This is the only place I ever loved,' he told her. They planned lunch for the following day: Hart, Porter and Pressly. Hart set to work the next morning, 'nipping at a bottle of tequila meanwhile'. Porter and Pressly were delayed, and Hart was furious. He gave the food to Daniel and sped into town for the embassy tea party, where he was promptly removed. He drank more, eventually showing up at Porter's gate to scream at her once again. This was the end of their friendship. The following day, an anonymous letter was sent to the secretary for the Mexican Minister of Education, Señor Jiménez. The complaint reached American diplomats and the Guggenheim Foundation.

C.A. died the day Hart received the telegram. By that time, Hart was on his way home. He had bought a plane ticket to Albuquerque – his first and only flight. From there, he made it to Ohio via the Santa Fe Railroad. Bessie delayed the funeral. She waited until 12 July to bury her husband, after Hart had made his long journey north.

Hart felt the loss 'more keenly' as a result of his visit with C.A. and Bessie the previous winter. He stayed for a month, helping 'Mrs Crane' with the settlement of the estate and offering her some comfort in her 'genuinely severe' grief. 'I'm so glad to *know* him before he died', he wrote '– it left me with a lot more self-respect than I had before'. Hart's thirty-second birthday passed on 21 July without remark. He stayed through August, and began to pack as the month drew to a close. Sáenz

131

wrote, calling him 'old scout' and updating him on his travels – he was off to Guatemala, so they would miss each other. 'It's such a shame you had to leave when we were getting acquainted,' Sáenz told him.

In September, Hart headed to New York, popping in to the Guggenheim Foundation to deliver a much-needed apology and another set of promises to curb his drinking. Waiting in the city for his crossing to Mexico, Hart ran into William Slater Brown in Washington Square. It was the last time the two friends would meet. In Slater Brown's memory, Hart had been 'hiding away from his friends'. He had no idea that Hart was in the city. They had lunch nearby. 'He asked me then if I thought he'd ever written anything of permanent value' . . . 'he seemed very depressed and in a sort of hopeless state of mind.' A few days later, Hart returned to Mexico on the *Orizaba*.

Arriving back at his low house in Mixcoac, the plants had been busy: 'the garden surprised me with its miraculous growth – sunflowers 14 foot high – profusion of roses, nasturtiums, violets, dahlias, cosmos, mignonette, etc . . .' He was relieved, finding comfort in the rainy season. It was long that year, but, Hart wrote, 'it keeps all the verdure so miraculously green that the countryside will hold its colors all the longer into the long months of drouth to come.'

Hart was in the centre of different forms of grief. His father's death was an unchosen loss, a shock coming just moments after Hart had received his last letter. A necessary choice: Hart had to 'completely break relations with Grace three years ago'. After she inherited his effects, Grace burned her attempts in letters and telegrams to reach her son during this period, and so I cannot reconstruct how she responded to Hart's need for space, but her anger and hurt is clear from her interviews with

Hart's biographers in the last years of her life. I cannot presume to know how Hart felt in the moment of his father's death, or the pain that he felt when Grace rejected him that night in Altadena.

I have sought out books where the adult writer reconstructs childhood memories, attempting to get a glimpse of an absent parent. Sparse documents, perhaps, and one or two photographs that might be combed over, again and again, mustering something out of nothing through writing about it: I did not know him, but perhaps I can conjure him here. But these are invariably accounts of a parent's death – a pain I cannot imagine and that surely must be worse than this. How, then, to look back through the eyes of that child, to create a portrait of the man who would decide, without explanation, I do not want you, I choose to lose you. But perhaps, for him, it was a gradual slipping away, a voice that fades on the wind.

Isla de la Juventud

There was a great deal to sort out. For a trip into the centre of the island, into the mountains, they would all need decent shoes. Leather. And trousers – canvas of some kind for the boys. She needed to book the car, too. Grace, C.A., and Harold (Hart), now fifteen, were staying on her mother's plantation on the Isle of Pines, Cuba.

The island has borne many names, after its parrots – Isla de Cotorras – and wealth of natural resources – *Tesoras*. Columbus seized the land for Spain in 1494, calling it La Evangelista and starting a period of colonisation, destabilising the native population. Under Fidel Castro's government, it became the Isla de la Juventud – Island of Youth.

Its history contains violence and restless ghosts. In the 1800s, Cuba held the largest enslaved population in Latin America; 800,000 people were held captive across its islands. Saidiya Hartman writes in *Lose Your Mother*, her memoir tracing the history of the Atlantic slave trade, that here Saint George was 'filled with gunpowder and blown up with a match'. His trials and the 'signs and symbols' of Saint George's 'world' were, she writes, 'first-hand knowledge' for the enslaved population.

There are suggestions that, perhaps, the Isle of Pines was Robert Louis Stevenson's *Treasure Island*, published in London three years before the US Congress passed the Thirteenth Amendment, abolishing slavery 'except as a punishment for crime' – an important, wrecking caveat.

For J. M. Barrie, perhaps Peter Pan's place of eternal child-hood, Neverland, might have been just thirty miles south of Cuba, across the Gulf of Batabanó, the largest island in an archipelago. Somewhere that was 'more or less an island, with astonishing splashes of colour here and there, and coral reefs and rakish-looking craft'.

The Hart plantation, Villa Casas, was in Nueva Gerona, the capital of the island. There were wide, palm-lined streets and houses with well-developed, mature gardens and buildings painted in bright colours: two shades of blue-green contrasted on pillars, set against a red-tiled roof, a church the colour of buttercups. Through their ownership of land on the island, the Harts expose one of the fault lines of neocolonialism in Latin America. The plantation was bought in the year of Grace and C.A.'s marriage. 'In plain view of the Caribbean sea', the Harts built a 'pleasant and commodious bungalow'. Around it was a large orange grove, with grapefruit and lemon trees. They spent the summers here, to avoid the 'long, cold winters of the north'.

The Isle of Pines was a forgotten colony, offering the United States a foothold in the region. Americans settled on the island in the late nineteenth century and set about importing goods, organising social clubs, and trying to establish the English language and the US dollar as the island's currencies. In 1925,

95 per cent of land on the island was owned by Americans. The United States had supported Cuba during the final stages of the war to win the island's independence from Spain in 1898. American support was self-interested, refusing to withdraw the troops sent to support the emerging republic until the position of US citizens on the Isle of Pines was guaranteed, a step on the way to annexation. In 1903 the United States and Cuba established the Hay–Quesada Treaty, acknowledging Cuban sovereignty over the island. The treaty was finally ratified in 1925, creating panic among the American settlers.

Grace liked to spend winters there, travelling alone after the death of her father, Clinton, in January 1913. In 1914 she and C.A. could not seem to stop arguing. And so it was decided that, this year, the whole family would travel, taking Harold out of school over the winter. In January 1915 they took the train from Ohio to Florida, staying overnight in Jacksonville. From there, they boarded a steamer for Cuba, then took another boat out to the island.

The holiday would do them good. They would find their way back to each other. That was, at least, the hope. But C.A. and Grace's troubles followed them. He refused to take a trip into the mountains. It was already mid-January. There was urgent business that required his presence in California. He was making a lot of money but he and Grace were spending a lot of time apart. She would not cancel the excursion into the mountains. Harold would love it, she was sure.

C.A. and Grace had an enormous row. He left immediately, Nueva Gerona to Cuba then on to Jacksonville in Florida. In Jacksonville he paused, distressed. He sat down at the cheap, wooden desk of the hotel and took out a pen. He could see her, dressed and ready to take the trip without him 'all the long way up the Coast'. There had been tears. She had told him they might never speak again. 'I can't tell you how I feel,' he wrote, 'I'm only ashamed of my weakness'. His heart pounded when he heard a telephone in the hallway, the sound seeming to bounce down the long corridor. C.A. hung on her moods, so did his son. They had travelled so far, only to find themselves in the same atmosphere, enclosed by Grace's shifting emotions. 'I'll drown my feelings the way only the weak do,' he told her.

Harold had begun to resemble his father, but with a shock of thick hair, which he wore combed upwards from his forehead. He was small, and his shoulders were still narrow and slightly sloping. It was his first trip out to the Hart plantation. He had heard a great number of stories about the place from his mother and grandmother. C.A. was concerned that Harold would miss too much school whereas Harold was convinced the trip would be somehow 'broadening'.

Grace had plans for them. They would see the wild centre of the island, beyond the town, taking walks into the mountains. Its heart was a tranche of swamp, with giant alligators and crabs scuttling through the marshes. The woods were dense with richly scented pine, cedar and mahogany. Close by, the island was sectioned into citrus farms. There were beaches, and friends to see at the clubs. Friends drifted in and out of the house. Grace couldn't stop talking. She felt uneasy. She wondered if, perhaps, she might be unwell. It could not be possible, she thought. Not here. She had been once, not so long ago. She was hospitalised when Harold was small, around nine, and sent to a sanatorium. It was the exhaustion of their separation, they said. She had just needed a long rest. She collapsed again after the divorce. That was 1917, just under a decade after the first break in their marriage.

She and C.A. had moved to Warren in 1901, six years before her mind unravelled. Warren was a large town a little way from Garrettsville. It was around this time that Clarence became 'C.A.' They took a new house: 407 North Park Avenue. Then they took another: 249 High Street, close to Hart's godmother, Aunt Zell (remarried to a newspaper man, William C. Deming). It would be easier to distribute the family's maple syrup from here, C.A. and Arthur decided (they produced 60,000 gallons a year). He was convinced they would make more money if they adulterated it, mixing it with corn syrup. It worked, and C.A. sold the business for a profit in 1908, the same year he and Grace first separated and she moved in with her parents in Cleveland. C.A. bought a new car and moved to Chicago. When Grace entered the sanatorium Harold remained with her parents. The Harts had moved from Chicago to Cleveland in 1903. He had a room in one of the house's two circular towers, overlooking the garden's cherry trees, with Lake Erie in the distance. The room was kept for him until his grandmother sold the house in 1925.

Back then, he started to read Dickinson, Whitman, Melville, Shakespeare, Baudelaire, and the Greenwich Village magazines, sent over from New York to Laukhuff's bookshop, which introduced him to the experiments of his contemporaries. He had a favourite chair, and would sit at the back of the store reading for hours. Slowly he started to write in his grandparents' tower room, finding a voice that, as the critic Langdon Hammer puts it, mixed 'emergent and vestigial styles', simultaneously modern and looking back to writers from previous generations.

Harold had been tiny when they moved to Warren, just three. He was barely walking. And C.A. was never there. Sometimes the boy couldn't stop crying. He cried until he made himself sick. Something was wrong now, Grace knew. His nausea had returned on the island. It was after C.A. left that Harold had started to feel unwell, she thought. He left so suddenly. She had been starting to gather their clothes for the trip, carefully packing their cases and finding clothes and shoes about the house to borrow. It was so embarrassing to have altered the reservation for the car. They had fought in public – everybody knew what had happened, and that he had left her. She would certainly make him wait. She would need, really, a good few weeks to get over the shock of it. The arguing made Harold sick. It was painful for him to recall this period as an adult.

After they returned from the mountains, Harold stole Grace's sleeping pills. He took them all. Another evening, he slit his wrists with a razor. Grace did not tell C.A. But she did write to ask him to confirm how many sleeping pills he had sent. She requested more. She couldn't sleep without them.

At first, Grace insisted that she and Harold would stay on the island until April, as planned. Eventually she relented, and C.A. made the journey south once again in order to escort his family back to Cleveland at the end of February. Harold disliked school but continued to read widely, discussing Voltaire, Swinburne, Byron, Poe and Wilde with a new friend, William Wright, who Hart first met at their Saturday dancing school on Euclid Avenue. Bill turned out to be a lifelong friend, with whom Hart swapped stories of travels and adventures, as well as sexual escapades and romances. In April 1915 Harold set out for Aurora, New York, where he attended a workshop by an unlikely friend of his father's, Elbert Hubbard, who was trying to establish a William Morris-style Arts and Crafts community of his own.

C.A.'s business had been going well. His Mary Garden Chocolates – named after the opera singer – were popular in Chicago, gracing the pantry of Harriet Moody, the widow of Professor William Vaughn Moody who ran a salon for artists and writers. Her friends included W. B. Yeats and Rabindranath Tagore as well as a local figure, Harriet Monroe, the founding editor of *Poetry* magazine. In a decade's time, Monroe would begin to publish Hart's poems. Harriet Moody read the young poet's attempts generously, offering advice and urging him to finish his schooling and attend university.

By the autumn of 1916, C.A. and Grace's marriage was over. The catalyst was C.A. taking a room at the Cleveland Athletic Club, moving some of his belongings from the Hart family home on East 115th Street. But the marriage was lost long before the trip to the island. Hart traced its dissolution back to a benefit concert a decade ago. He was eight. Grace had been engaged to sing at the event. C.A. had tried to intervene, apparently embarrassed, though her voice had been so praised during their courtship. In the end, he left noisily, his chair scraping, as she walked across the stage. Six years later in the poem 'Porphyro in Akron', Hart took up his father's voice:

> Your mother sang that in a stuffy parlour
> One summer day in a little town
> Where you had started to grow.
> And you were outside as soon as you
> Could get away from the company
> To find the only rose on the bush
> In the front yard . . .

Hart escaped to the Village as the new year opened 1917. His parents' divorce was finalised in April. Hart had already started to publish, with short poems appearing in the magazines run from offices around Washington Square. In his case he had a copy of the Bible and Mary Baker Eddy's *Science and Health with Key to the Scriptures*. Grace followed Hart to New York in May, taking an apartment with her mother close to Gramercy Park. Grace and C.A. began writing to each other. They toyed with a reunion, even planning a second marriage. But they consistently argued over Hart's prospects and Grace's psychological health was worsening. C.A. rebuffed her. Grace suffered a serious and extended breakdown in August, culminating in a suicide attempt. She took bichloride of mercury in the hope that it was enough to kill her. It wasn't, of course. In September she moved back to Cleveland with her mother. Hart joined them, taking a job in a munitions factory (he lasted a month). The effects of Grace's breakdown dragged into 1918, with a relapse in March. C.A., meanwhile, was making wedding plans. He celebrated his marriage to Frances Kelly that August.

With Waldo Frank in tow, Hart returned to the Isle of Pines a decade after his first visit. He was twenty-five, and trying to work on *The Bridge*. His living expenses would be about a third cheaper than in New York, buying him time to write. On 3 May 1926, the *Orizaba* was sailing just off the Florida coast. Beyond the prow he could see flying fish springing from the waves and 'the usual increasing blue' of the sea. On 4 May, the ship docked in Havana. 'The whole town is hyper-sensual and mad – i.e. has no apparent direction, destiny, or purpose', he wrote. 'I shall have to go up for a real spree sometime when cash is plentiful, meanwhile this isle is enough Eden.' With the help of Frank's Spanish, they explored 'off all beaten paths', avoiding the 'American cafes' as the two passed from cafe to cafe drinking 'marvellous sherry, cognac, vermouth and "Tropical"', a beer, and buying lottery tickets.

They went along past 'gratings and balconies and narrow streets with plenty of whores nodding.' The alcohol and cigars were expensive. They visited a burlesque, which even Hart found 'broad' (the view he had of 'outspoken buttocks' would find its way into *The Bridge*). A fleet of American destroyers had arrived at the port, but cruising sailors was an impossibility with the ascetic Frank at his side. He could watch, at least, the 'torrents of uniforms' – men in white sailor suits and hats at all angles walked through the decaying streets, the odd flash of ankle above trousers worn slightly too short and tight over the bottom, tops that skimmed the hips with navy ties hanging at a diagonal, accentuating the hardness of the chest. Hart was half looking out for an old 'jack tar friend', described only as 'J.F.' in letters. J.F.'s ship passed by Cuba and on to New York without stopping.

Hart and Waldo arrived on the Isle of Pines on 5 May. Hart was reunited with Mrs T. W. ('Sally') Simpson, the Villa Casas caretaker. A resident on the island described her as 'a little, dried-up, sun wrinkled wisp of a woman with sharp (dark?) eyes behind glasses, an active mind and an acid tongue and a warm heart.' Hart adored her, calling her Aunt Sally. Their friendship survived the rest of Hart's life as Aunt Sally stepped into something resembling a maternal role after Hart's relationship with Grace was severed in 1928. Hart included Aunt Sally in *The Bridge*, as part of his own monologue in 'The River', in which he also dwells on his 'father's cannery works', and the 'rail squatters' that sat behind that symbol of C.A.'s increasing wealth.

Aunt Sally put Hart in Grace's old room, with Waldo next door. There was a mango tree visible from the window, a 'Sun-heap' with 'gay spiders . . . silking of shadows good underdrawers for owls'. The idea that the spiders spun fabric, like silkworms, was a flight of fancy, but the owl was real. Hart and Waldo rescued the bird, which squawked through the house. The pair ate tropical fruits and legged up trees to pick coconuts. They went to markets and cooked fish straight off the boat and swam, the water soothing their mosquito bites. The buildings on the island were white, gold and azure – almost too pretty for Hart, who found the towns 'insipid'. 'Even plaster has something to say', he wrote. Memories of the last trip pressed upon Hart. 'My memory I left in a ravine', he wrote in a new poem, 'Passage', thinking both of his suicide attempts and the arguments ('icy speeches') between his parents.

Waldo left after two weeks, recording his impressions of the island in an essay, 'Habana of the Cubans'. Hart stayed awhile. Property prices were falling with the knowledge that the Cuban government was now legally able to requisition the land occupied by American settlers. Nearby, a prison was being built. In the 1950s it would house Fidel Castro. Raised in rose-gold brick, the prison's panopticon design enabled each guard based in a turret at the centre of one of the three buildings to watch over 1,000 inmates. The model offered a perfect view of the prisoners' cells, which formed a single honeycombed layer wrapped around the external wall. 'Visibility is a trap', wrote Michel Foucault of the design phenomenon, finding in it a metaphor for the internalisation of the mores of a censorious society.

Hart had intended to spend his time working on *The Bridge*. As a teenager, he had toyed with writing a novel about the islanders, but abandoned the idea hastily after his mother disapproved. Work on the long poem was slow, but he composed a remarkable set of poems about the island, including 'Passage', 'The Mango Tree', 'Island Quarry' and a poem for his mother, 'Royal Palm', which addresses Grace's frustrated ambitions: 'Forever fruitless', 'our deathward breath is sealed – ' he writes. He imagines how she might climb up a palm tree 'Unshackled, casual of its azured height / As though it soared suchwise through heaven too.'

The storms came in June. Hart was kept busy securing the house and fielding bowls full of water leaking through the roof. He arranged a trip to Grand Cayman, hoping for fresh inspiration to write. The voyage was horrendous, with clouds of mosquitos descending on the ship and the sea 'a blinding, glassy gridiron'. He read *Moby Dick* for a third time, locked inside his rooms on the island for ten days. His letters home are foul and racist diatribes, taking his rage out on fellow passengers on the boat and the inhabitants of the island. Arriving back at Villa Casas, he was so badly sunburned that lesions had emerged on his skin and abscesses had formed in each ear. His throat was infected from unclean water. Still, the result was two new poems, 'The Hurricane' and 'The Air Plant'.

With the energy of two completed lyrics, work on *The Bridge* resumed. 'I feel an absolute music in the air again,' he wrote to Waldo in July, 'some tremendous rondure floating somewhere.' There is a touch of Caliban in these comments, to whom Shakespeare gives some of the most beautiful lines in *The Tempest*. The play is set on an island that mingles Mediterranean and Caribbean qualities, overseen by Prospero, coloniser magician. Caliban is native to the island, taught English by Prospero and his daughter, Miranda. Addressing two newcomers, Stephano and Trinculo, Caliban soothes them: 'Be not afeard; the isle is full of noises, / Sounds and sweet airs, that give delight and hurt not'. Hart, as Caliban, imagines himself taught music and rhythm by the island.

Hart finished 'To Brooklyn Bridge' not in his bedroom overlooking the structure but some 2,000 kilometres away, using his memories to, as he put it, 'lend a myth to god', and construct its soaring wires on the page. More naturally, he started work on 'Cutty Sark', his hymn to drunken sailors. 'No – I can't live on land – !', shouts one in a Manhattan bar, before the poet walks home to Brooklyn, finding his way across the same, glimpsing at the Statue of Liberty and 'that torch of hers'. Next: 'The Tunnel', where he descended into the New York Subway and tried to reckon with the 'damned dead' world of T. S. Eliot's *The Waste Land*, a poem which both inspired and shook him with its brilliance. He wanted – and would – counter Eliot's pessimism in *The Bridge*, through movements from the subterranean underworld of the city, glorying in its dirt and eroticism as men cruise by the piers, and voices on the trains shift into the rhythms of jazz, and up through architectural flights. He was '*completely*' in his work, where 'every circumstance and incident in one's life flocks towards a positive centre of action, control and beauty.' He was listening to the island, but the sounds were pleasant, urging him on. 'You can hear the very snakes rejoice', he told Waldo, 'the long shaken-out convulsions of rock and roots.' By August, he had the architecture of the poem, with key sections in draft or carefully planned. He would take a break in Havana. In Havana he met another sailor, Alfredo, whose ship was the *Maximo Gomez*.

In October, a terrible storm came. Aunt Sally and Hart lay under the bed with the house dog Attaboy. All around them, they could hear chunks of plaster falling from the ceilings, walls splitting and gables sheared in two. During a moment of respite, Hart strode out into the garden naked, spied by Aunt Sally who remembered 'Adonis striding through the tall grass garbed "a la naturel"'. She wondered 'how we both came out so well.' In town, buildings were razed, flooded, on fire. There were two hundred dead floating in the harbour. Six hundred died within Cuba's bounds. Hart recorded the attempt to save the house in a poem, 'Eternity'.

> We shovelled and sweated; watched the ogre sun
> Blister the mountain, stripped now, bare of palm

Destroyers came and Hart eyed the sailors and drank Bacardi with them in a bar called Mack's. Villa Casas was a ruin. Aunt Sally lent Hart the money to return home. That last week, he took Veronal to sleep. He made his way home via Havana, where he sought out Alfredo. The search was fruitless; Alfredo had suffered great injuries during the storm – the *Maximo Gomez* had sunk.

And now, fifteen years later, Grace was polishing tables and living between evenings with Frances. She found herself stuck, her thoughts circular and winding in on themselves. Perhaps if she kept writing and recording, these memories might lessen their pressure upon her. 'Memory, committed to the page, had broke', Hart wrote in 'Passage', those 'piteous admissions to be split / Upon the page'. The poem a 'Record of rage and partial appetites' – hers, she thought. He meant hers.

12

Tepoztlán

In Diego Rivera's imagination, Tepoztlán is glimpsed through three maguey plants. Rockets explode across the composition, with a cathedral and a *pulquería* nestled in the town beneath stepped columns of rock north of the settlement. Rivera compresses several fields of vision so that the Temple of Tepozteco can be seen from this vantage point: the ruins are suggested in the squared-off lines of the cliffs in the background, beyond the maguey.

The town sits south of Mexico City in the Morelos region on the edge of a vast forest and the copper-dipped Sierra de Tepoztlán mountain range. It holds a famous annual festival after its namesake Ometochtli Tepoztēcatl, an Aztec god who presided over the wind, crops, and pulque, honoured with ritualised drinking. Tepoztēcatl was one of the Centzon Tōtōchtin, four hundred gods born of the union between Mayahuel and Patecatl, the goddess of the maguey and the god-discoverer of fermentation. These gods were associated with rabbits, partially, it is said, because of their fertility, partially because rabbits lived among the magueys. In one Aztec legend, pulque was discovered by a rabbit who accidentally scratched at the centre of a maguey with a sharp claw. It drank the juice. It liked it and returned, day after day, finding it fermented.

Hart spent a week in Tepoztlán in September 1931, just days after arriving back at Mexico City. The trip was arranged by a new friend, Milton Rourke, a young archaeologist from Wisconsin who, unlike Hart, spoke Spanish. Milton stayed with Hart regularly after the trip. A mutual friend described him as 'a queer, a fuzzy Marxist, and a sponger, all in one.' Milton was convinced there was a buried Aztec pyramid under Hart's house. Hart liked him.

Hart had returned to Mexico hoping to get back to his work. To do so, he needed to extend his travels and move beyond, as he put it, 'the more artificial contacts that museums proffer'. Porter tried to access Mexican culture through reading and research. Hart, without Spanish, hoped to gain knowledge through experience, travelling, visiting festivals and local artists. 'I came back with the resolution to get more into the smaller cities and pueblos, to get as thoroughly acquainted with the native Indian population as possible', he explained.

Milton took Hart out on digs, taking picks and shovels and shredding into the sides of abandoned villages in the hills overlooking Anahuac, the valley known as the basin of Mexico that encircles Mexico City. From one site, a settlement deserted during the conquest, Hart could see two great volcanoes on the horizon. The valley was 'glazed' by Lake Texcoco, 'seemingly below which floats, as in a dream, the City of Mexico'. It was 'haunting and melancholy'. The picks raised untouched earth and released a 'grassy perfume' as well as shards of pottery and a sharp fragment of obsidian that, Milton guessed, was part of a knife. 'It is still a mystery as to how they cut obsidian', wrote Hart to Sam, 'but this shard was perfectly edged and graded as though it had been conformable as wood.'

Milton and Hart took a train from Mexico City, and travelled four hours south, stopping an afternoon's hike from Tepoztlán. Hart and Milton walked for three miles and then began their descent into a valley. They passed cliffs 'as high as 800 feet', with 'basalt ledges with a perilous sheer drop' covered in 'dense tropical foliage and veritable hanging gardens – with cascades and waterfalls galore'. They arrived at a town surrounded by cornfields, rich, so Milton told Hart, with buried Aztec idols. Hart had Milton as his guide, as well as his treasured copy of Anita Brenner, and anthropological studies by two Americans, Carleton Beals (*Mexican Maze*) and Stuart Chase (*Mexico*). Hart was so eager to make the trip that he was prepared to sleep on the floor of the ruined monastery. It was the eve of the town's festival, the Feast Day of the Nativity of the Blessed Virgin Mary, celebrated on 8 September.

Hart and Milton stumbled through Tepoztlán's rough stone streets, making their way to the monastery, the Convento de la Natividad – a version of which appears in Malcolm Lowry's *Under the Volcano*. In 1521 Cortés burned Tepoztlán to the ground, ruining Tepozteco's temple. It still clung to the side of a cliff, Hart wrote, 'confronting the town'. A monastery was eventually commissioned, built between 1555 and 1580. It would house an inquisitor. Under the eyes of a Dominican order, Indigenous Tepoztecos laid the carved stones, sandwiched with lime and sand. Intricate patterns were painted on the interior walls: crosses and kings and saints circled with leaves, the Virgin and the order's emblem: a dog bearing a lit torch.

Hart and Milton climbed up the stairs and onto the roof of the cathedral. Around twenty-five locals had gathered, dressed in simple white suits and hats. A second group waited for sunrise in the old temple, spending the night looking down and over the cathedral below. There were lit lanterns scattered across the roof. The bells rang loudly, swung by the church sextons. They would find their way into Hart's final poem (later translated by Octavio Paz), 'The Broken Tower'. Mingled with church bells he could hear as he worked on the poem while lying in bed in Taxco, he imagined the din made that 'vocal morning' in Tepoztlán, and the 'bell rope that gathers God at dawn', swung by their 'sexton slave'.

In their brief gaps between peals, a flute player and drummer made music, facing up to the old temple. Hart heard a performance of two voices in conflict, 'the idol's and the Cross'. But, he wrote, 'there really did not seem to be a real conflict that amazing night'. And anyway, he added, 'Nearly all of these "elders" I have been describing go to mass!' The two traditions had mixed over centuries. Aztec rituals shifted out into rural areas like Tepoztlán as Christianity spread – into the hills and caves. Christian feast days were adapted to mark the ancient passages of the two seasons (wet and dry), with rituals of rain and maize enmeshed in the Christian calendar, as in the Feast Day of the Virgin.

Hart and Milton sat on the roof listening to stories. The locals explained the old myths to the two Americans, with Milton translating for Hart. Tepoztécatl was born to an Indigenous virgin. She bathed in a pool where there lived a spirit, disguised as a small bird. She found herself pregnant with Tepoztécatl, who was cast out by her family. He was adopted by an old man who lived near Mazacuatl, a snake who fed on the elderly. When it was his father's turn, Tepoztécatl took his place. The snake ate Tepoztécatl, who then sliced himself out of the snake's belly with a piece of obsidian. Lightning scanned the eastern horizon and a crescent moon descended in the west. The sky was lit with stars. 'It truly was the Land of Oz', Hart wrote, 'with the high valley walls in the Wizard's circle.' Rockets soared around, whizzing in conversation between the cathedral and the temple.

At nine, the music stopped and Hart, Milton and the elders made their way to a stall, where Hart bought round after round of tequila. The elders invited Hart and Milton to join them for the 'conclusion of the watch', early the next morning.

Hart and Milton paused for a few hours, sharing a bamboo bed in a baker's house. They overslept slightly, waking at five in the morning to 'the weird notes of drum and fife in the dark valley'. They walked back through the dark, narrow streets and, once again, up into the cathedral. The two men stepped onto the roof as the sun started to lift over a break in the cliffs to the east. The damp air smelled faintly of alcohol and rocket smoke. The same group of elders offered them both coffee: hot and cloudy with pulque.

A drum had been set out, brought down from the temple while Hart and Milton were in bed. Laid out on the stone, the elders explained that it was an ancient Aztec drum, made pre-conquest. It was 'guarded year after year from the destruction of the priests and conquerors', 'beaten to propitiate the god' many hundreds of times. The drum was a large cylinder with a figure with an animal head carved into the wood. The figure was upright, 'walking through thick woods'. Two Indigenous musicians sat cross-legged with padded batons, slowly beating the drum as the sun rose.

The drumbeats sped up as the sun began to climb and leak through the gap in the hills. One of the drummers turned to Hart and passed him the baton. He was amazed to be invited to participate, having felt grateful for the evening before, when he and Milton had been able to sit and watch the festivities. 'I not only beat the exact rhythm with all due accents, which they had been keeping up for hours', Hart told Bill Wright, but, typically, he deviated, and 'even worked in an elaboration, based on the lighter tattoo of the more modern drama of the evening before.' It was tiring, exhausting the muscles in his arms. At six, he and the musicians embraced, walking in step from side to side of the cathedral in a brief dance. The sextons wielded their hammers, swinging on the bells with their full weight 'like frantic acrobats', while another round of rockets flew into the air.

The rest of the days passed quickly: he bathed in mountain streams with a young Indigenous man, and ate beans and tortillas. He and Milton walked out to the cornfields, digging until they uncovered idols in the soil. On their final day, the two made the steep climb up to Tepozteco's temple, north of the town. They passed the cathedral where the vicar, Hart quipped, was 'at stool', praying on his knees. Further on, in a place called the Axitla, a small spring emerges from the mountain. The temple at the top was constructed by the Xochimilca people in the twelfth and thirteenth centuries. This was a sacred site, a journey's end for pilgrims, carrying offerings of rubber, flowers, and pulque.

When Hart visited, the temple still had fragments with visible relief cut into the stone. It was 'staunchly and beautifully constructed', wrote Hart, with grey wedges of stone forming a ten-metre pyramid on a broad platform, with steps sweeping up its left side and all surrounded by green foliage. Hart took a photograph from the hillside, his view down onto the cathedral interrupted by palm fronds.

Hart and Milton took the train back to Mexico City to join the celebrations that surrounded Mexican Independence Day on 16 September, where there would be parties and tableaux and performances across a few days. Hart recorded the trip in a long letter after the two arrived home – one of the most detailed and vibrant pieces of writing that survives from his time in Mexico. 'I have never left a town feeling so mellow and in such pleasant relations with everybody in the place', he wrote. He would return soon, he decided.

13

Siqueiros Comes to Stay

On a small block of wood, David Alfaro Siqueiros chiselled the outline of a woman holding a child. Her shape was formed from etched flanks of light and shadow, with the child bundled at her front. Her feet were set apart. She looked like she was waiting. Siqueiros completed a series of thirteen woodcut reliefs while in Lecumberri Prison. Known as the Black Palace, Lecumberri was in the north-east of Mexico City, and is now the home of Mexico's National Archives. Imprisoned in May 1930, Siqueiros was not released until November. He returned to its walls in 1960, once again as a political prisoner.

Wanted for his association with the banned Communist Party, Siqueiros – founder of the National Union of Revolutionary Painters, Sculptors and Engravers and a former captain in General Álvaro Obregón's forces – was captured while marching in the Worker's Parade on May Day, 1930. During the same round-up, the American photographer Tina

Modotti (a close friend of Frida Kahlo's) was also captured and deported to Germany. According to his biographer, Siqueiros was sent to Lecumberri 'without warrant or charge'. The dummy President, Pascual Ortiz Rubio (in turn governed by *el Jefe Máximo* Plutarco Elías Calles), had just survived an assassination attempt: a shot to the mouth. This offered the government an excuse to crack down on members and associates of the Communist Party, whether or not it was behind the attack.

Siqueiros spent ten days of his sentence in solitary confinement. 'My dinner was served to me in the lower part of my sweater,' he remembered later, explaining that he had to stretch out the fabric to 'receive' his food each night. He was cold. There was no coffee (unless, he was told, he was prepared to take that, too, in his cupped hands). He was badly beaten inside his cell by a group of jailors, provoked by his request for the blankets that his wife, the poet Blanca Luz Brum, had left for him.

Brum took a bus from the city out to the Black Palace to see her husband. She felt isolated; neither the Party nor their artist-friends could help her, fearing any association with Siqueiros. She was struggling to feed herself and her son, Eduardo. She could not find buyers for Siqueiros's paintings; 'Not until he abandons his ideas!' she was told. She wrote to Siqueiros insistently, gradually forming her own record of the six months. 'I don't understand your indignation this morning. I thought you would embrace me madly when you saw me', she writes one day; 'To see your head so bowed and sad rips me', she wrote on another. Later, she gathered her letters together, naming the collection after the bus that had carried her *Penitenciaria, Niño Perdido* (*Penitentiary, Lost Child*). The book was introduced by the writer Eugene Jolas in Paris, who happened to be a friend of Hart's. Her writing is 'restless', wrote Jolas, 'casting its gaze on all of humanity'.

Siqueiros needed his own record of his imprisonment. Brum provided him with a few basic materials. Siqueiros carved shapes into short fragments of wood that, when inked, formed hammers and anvils, workers and prisoners, soldiers and revolutionaries, women by a railroad track. Watching and looking are themes. Government troops and rebels switch positions: they gather in defence, for a battle, or an incursion, or they observe these movements from a vantage point. Two workers, each carrying a child, stare forward out of the print. A profile looms out of the bar-like lines of shadow that edge the page, watching the couple.

After his release in November 1930, Siqueiros and Brum were forced into inner exile in Taxco until April 1932. Siqueiros began to conceive of the series of Lecumberri prints as a book; Brum worked on her manuscript of letters. Siqueiros printed the woodcuts on orange paper and arranged them into a volume, *13 Grabados*. William Spratling, his friend and neighbour, wrote an introduction for the book. Spratling found 'cumulative force' in the 'profound and basic' forms of the woodcuts, with their repeated shapes and motifs. '[T]he surface of a small woodblock may be made as intense and dramatic as a whole play', he wrote. But they also seemed to show whole worlds of suffering and rebellion in miniature, through just a few shapes assembled together. Just as, as Spratling put it, a play or novel might capture 'the whole of itself in a single gesture', like Cornwall taking Gloucester's eyes in *King Lear*, or Dorian Gray stabbing his own portrait. Spratling, a silversmith, focuses on the forms of the woodblocks, not just the prints that they produced. The blocks are art objects, testament both to Siqueiros's artistic process and his time in jail. Carved during the painter's incarceration, personal and political history are contained within the chiselled wood, traces of it lingering, reproduced in each print.

Siqueiros and Brum found a house high up in the Taxco hills. They hung a lantern shaped like a large red star from their porch. A circle formed in Taxco, with Siqueiros, Brum, Spratling, Anita Brenner, Porter, Sáenz, and Hart. George Gershwin dropped in, as did Sergei Eisenstein, who was filming in Mexico. The American artist and writer Ione Robinson visited. She was researching the muralists, and would record Siqueiros and Brum's life in Taxco in a book called *A Wall to Paint On*, which would take her over a decade to complete.

Spratling, Sáenz and Hart sat for portraits by their friend. Siqueiros's portraits of Spratling and Sáenz almost appear as a pair: black-and-white lithographs, the heads of both men turned slightly to their left shoulders. Spratling seems to return Siqueiros's gaze, Sáenz avoids it, appearing almost to look over the painter's shoulder about to answer a question or offer a greeting or farewell. Based on pre-Columbian Olmec heads that were hewn from basalt boulders about two or three metres tall, Siqueiros carved those of his friends from layers of greasy pigment, monoliths flattened into two dimensions. Both are now in collections at MOMA in New York.

As well as his portrait, painted during a series of sittings that autumn, Hart bought two small studies by Siqueiros. On the same trip to Taxco, he acquired a dozen 'small watercolours' by local children (none of which could have been older than eight, he noted), all landscapes, for about twenty cents each. He had overspent, assuming his inheritance from his father's estate would be more generous. In fact, he had a handful of dollars left to last him from November to January.

Hart's letters record his first impressions of Siqueiros's work, fully articulated in an essay accompanying Siqueiros's first solo exhibition in Mexico City the following January. Like Spratling, Hart was amazed at the miniature worlds contained in Siqueiros's small studies. 'He's fundamentally a mural painter', he wrote, but 'even his smaller paintings have tremendous *scale*.' Hart was thinking of how a muralist might begin with small studies, which then found their way into large, expansive wall paintings so vast in composition that the eye copes by moving from detail to detail. In *América Tropical*, painted in LA in 1932, the eye rests, perhaps, on a vulture perched on a branch. Or just the branch itself, generously curved and reaching towards an Indigenous figure, crucified and presided over by an eagle.

Hart was interested in how artworks can be structured, divided into sections and scenes. The first analogy Hart had found for this was Cubism, where the traditional, single vantage point is rejected in favour of multiple perspectives. With this in mind, he wrote long poems that could be divided into parts, rearranged and reformulated. The sections could be read independently as discrete lyrics and studies. He published the sections of *The Bridge* separately in magazines, but he also explains the process in its final poem, 'Atlantis'. The poem forms a 'star', Hart wrote, while its individual sections are like 'spears ensanguined', drawn from it, bloody with the traces of ideas. They can be read independently, but they also 'leap and converge' into 'one song' when read as a whole.

The muralists pushed his thinking beyond the aesthetic play of writing and then breaking his own works into fragments.

My guess is that 'Nopal' was a short study that was destined to be included in a sprawling, fractured long poem. We have some clues from the slips of paper Hart left behind and from his letters: the eyes would rest a moment on the nopal, before shifting to the *Orizaba* and Zinsser tipping the rats overboard, to Cortés landing at Tabasco.

Although Hart destroyed his own portrait, photographs of it survive. Rendered in black and white by the camera, and much smaller than its original dimensions (four feet by two), Hart leans with one arm laid over the other. Siqueiros places us – looking at him looking at Hart – opposite Hart at a table. Or it could be a bar; the view is foreshortened, with the rims of glasses below Hart's wrists. Siqueiros's version of Hart is all angles, the planes of the face constructed in broad wedges. The eyes look to his hands, which are perhaps even closed. The photograph might have cropped the composition, but Hart's body barely seems contained by the canvas. He fills it claustrophobically, at once crushed and bursting out of the frame.

The shine on the glossy square on the table makes the image move. At times he seems to shift from his stupor, caught in a moment before he blinks and looks up, with the twitch beginning at the corner of the mouth. Hart slashed the portrait with his father's razor just weeks before he died. His pretext was that the paint was cheap and starting to crack. But he began by slicing through his own eyes.

Luckily, Hart sent copies of the photograph to friends, including Sam. The photograph before me lives in an archive in New York, like the portraits of his friends. Because it is a proxy for the destroyed work, the photograph represents a moment of self-destruction. As such, it seems strange to find it numbered and in its own manila file among pictures of friends, lovers, pamphlets, newspaper clippings, letters – the detritus that I am now using to try to reconstruct his life. When I first pull out the print I half expect to find it maimed, with Hart sightless as the photograph mimics the painting's first wound. I wonder if anyone has ever been tempted to take out their pencil and run the sharp lead across his lowered brow.

I put the photograph back in the envelope. I was tired. It was December 2013 and I had travelled up from Washington DC, where I had a fellowship at the Library of Congress as part of my doctoral studies. I was staying in the Seafarer's Mission in Union Square, sleeping in a bed draped in a dusty pink floral spread and using a shared shower covered in the pubic hair of the giant, polite men I rode with in the lift. I was broke, thanks to a bank fraud that had yet to be resolved. I sat on the hotel bed almost every evening. But on Wednesday I walked alone across Brooklyn Bridge in the dark. I thought of Hart and Emil, 'walking hand in hand across the most beautiful bridge in the world' with, Hart wrote, 'the cables enclosing us and pulling us upwards in such a dance as I have never walked and never can walk with another.' I found a picture of Emil that day, alongside the Siqueiros portrait. He was blond and impossibly beautiful, muscled in a spotless sailor's vest and trousers, barefoot on Hart's rooftop at Columbia Heights, the bridge behind him.

That afternoon I packed away my pencils and stuffed my notes in my bag and caught the Greyhound back to D.C. I sat next to a woman talking loudly – I assumed on the phone. When we arrived, I realised the conversation had been with herself. I walked back to my dormitory, a barred room in Thompson-Markward Hall. The residents (many of them aides and likely future politicians) took part in a strange daily burlesque. In the large bathroom, they insisted on walking into the showers fully dressed, flinging their clothes over the shower curtains once safely inside. One morning a pair of trainers flew past my head, the rubber smacking the greying tiles. I took this as a provocation, and stripped off in the centre of the room, leaving my towel on the bench behind me.

I didn't know it, but I had walked through New York on a broken ankle after falling down a flight of stairs. I felt twinges while I was in the archives, flicking through the files, and a sharper pain when I stood to photograph particular items. It was only after I returned to the UK, where I was studying for my PhD at Durham University, and had another fall that I thought to go to hospital. It turned out that I had freshly broken my left foot, while my right ankle had begun to mend without intervention. 'Did you throw yourself down the stairs?' the consultant asked. 'Throw?' I thought. Odd. Worse than to leap or to jump? 'No,' I said. Two clacks on the keyboard. 'You're an outpatient with the psychiatric ward. So we have to ask. I'm sorry.' 'I get it,' I said, 'I would ask me too.' I restrained myself from further explanations. I had learned from conversations with my psychologist that I could choose when to unspool my personal and medical histories. It had never occurred to me that some questions did not need answering (the poet Marianne Moore has a useful phrase: 'omissions are not accidents').

The consultant leaned forward and smiled, the kind without teeth that enlarges the chin and raises the eyebrows up and out towards the ears. 'In future, please come straight in. It looks like you might be having trouble assessing your own pain levels.' We looked at the X-rays. There was a wide space between the far-left bones of my left foot, the metatarsal. I thought of my socks, my apple-green trainers pressing into the gap, the tarmac, and I felt sick. The nurse squeezed my shoulder and trimmed my jeans to the knee, encasing my foot and shin in bright orange plaster.

On 15 November 1931, Siqueiros and Brum arrived at Hart's home in Mixcoac, doctors in tow. While Hart was a little rundown with flu and the effects of the drink, Siqueiros was suffering with malaria. He had to be carried into the house. He was 'deathly ill', wrote Hart, following eight days of mounting fever. 'There was nothing to do but rush to Mexico City,' Hart told Sam. 'I'm glad to be of help in such a crisis.' He anticipated that Siqueiros and Brum would need to stay for a few months. It was a good arrangement, for the time being, 'and since I had three rooms which I never used the house really isn't crowded.'

Hart was delighted to welcome 'the greatest painter in Mexico'. He took a photograph of the couple: Brum's hair pulled back into a beret, her hand resting on her husband's shoulder, half smiling at Hart. Siqueiros is striking: his eyebrows pinched together as he looks at the camera, his dark, wavy hair scooped backwards from one ear. Hart threw the invalid parties and dinners. Through Siqueiros and Brum, Hart made a new friend, Lisa, a friend of the couple's. He had a new companion for dancing and drinking tequila. Lisa stayed in the house for free until Hart left Mexico, cooking and cleaning in exchange.

Hart had spent the first days of November immersing himself in the festivities of the Day of the Dead. That immersion meant drinking a great deal and watching local rituals. He went to the cemetery, where he saw families 'sitting on tombstones day and night holding lighted candles to the spirits of the dead'. They brought food and drink and, as Hart recalled, it was 'far from being sad, it's very merry'. There were firecrackers in the image of Judas and skeleton toys made from paper and clay. He wandered the city, visiting markets set up in a park in the city. 'A walk through there beats the excitement of any museum I've ever been in', he wrote, in one of many diary-like letters sent to two of his old friends back in Cleveland: the Czech-born set and costume designer Richard Rychtarik and his wife, Charlotte, a talented pianist. Prior to Siqueiros and Brum's arrival, Hart had enjoyed a period of parties. His parties were large and dozens of guests would mill in and out of the house over the course of an evening. Daniel, who was a fine guitarist and singer, would bring friends to play music 'as would make your feet dance and your eyes shine brightly'. The parties often descended into chaos. A few weeks before, one had grown a 'little too lively' even for Hart when an American tourist drank a quart of tequila and climbed onto Hart's neighbour's house and began peeling off the tiles, using them as missiles to pelt the other guests below.

Between socialising and Siqueiros's illness, the house began to feel crowded. His guests, as entertaining as they might have been, became exhausting. Caring for Siqueiros required attention to 'thousands of details', with visitors and doctors' appointments, and extra work and errands required by the servants that 'naturally disorganised the quiet routine of the household completely'. Siqueiros and Brum had a constant stream of visitors: doctors, Party members, other artists and writers. The house was bedlam for Hart; too much noise and arguments about the minutiae of Marxist principles, with Milton Rourke translating for Hart. Lesley Simpson claimed that Hart turned to him for support. Simpson said that Hart referred to his guests as 'cockeyed communists'. 'By God, I love you – you're so damned *middle class*', Simpson recalled Hart declaring one night after he 'rescued him from his household'. 'I'm middle class too,' said Hart, apparently. 'The only people who ever did anything were middle class.'

There are no traces of these comments in Hart's letters, or any like them. This is not to say that he didn't say them, or say parts of them. But what he did describe was the lack of control he felt during Siqueiros and Brum's visit. Given Modotti's expulsion from Mexico, perhaps he regretted the impulsive decision to host the couple; they had wired him a panicked telegram shortly before setting out from Taxco, desperate for a base for medical care. Hart was known to the local police, and had been threatened with deportation for his consistent anti-social behaviour.

Hart needed to escape. He packed his things and headed back to Tepoztlán. A long walk through the mountains would clear his head.

14

A Seance in New York

Grace was surprised by the conventions of the seance. These events started like any other meeting, with a great deal of prevarication. It was early June 1941; she and Frances had met dozens of times by now. On each occasion, the time was padded out with odd bureaucracies and explanations – and money, of course. It had its own terminology, scripts and private language. That, at least, was somewhat familiar. She had learned various things that she believed when it suited her. And what is faith but a moving thing, unchanged by – defined even – by its moving. There was the idea that, as the founder of the Christian Science movement Mary Baker Eddy wrote, 'man dies not'. He dies not; he did not die. Universal death is a fiction. Life is untouched by disease. As Frances declared in one of her trances, after death the spirit exists 'minus the physical elements of earth . . . Real and incorruptible'. Easier to believe for Grace when her back wasn't out, or her throat wasn't catching with the mould behind the wallpaper.

Hart had no patience with the Christian Scientists, though he indulged Grace a little as a boy. She did smile, though, when she saw fragments of Mary Baker Eddy's service book, the *Christian Science Hymnal*, start to emerge in poems. In 'The Wine Menagerie', in which we find a voice (Hart's, really) propping up a dive bar in New York, Hart rushes through a confusion of images, drawing on half-remembered hymns, biblical stories, Baudelaire, Stravinsky – incoherent ramblings. He plays on lines by Isaac Watts from Eddy's *Hymnal*: 'Not from dust affliction grows . . . Yet we are born to care and woes / A sad inheritance'. Hart twists this into 'Though in the end you know / And count some dim inheritance of sand, / How much yet meets the treason of the snow'. A 'sad' inheritance turns 'dim'. Hart could hear the music of the hymn as he wrote, taking Watts's couplet of 'woes / know' and rhyming with it insistently.

Grace's grandmother would soothe her in the early hours when she was a child. It was a mystery as to why she would tumble from her bed in the night and walk. The feel of the boards and the rugs usually woke her, tears streaming down her face. She couldn't quite describe what she saw: sometimes a presence at the foot of the bed, sometimes she was trapped, jumping from strange platforms on and on, as far as she could see. Her grandmother, a thick robe draped around her shoulders, would lift her back into the bedclothes. 'If a person wouldn't harm you when they were alive, why would they do it once they've passed?' her grandmother would say, half serious. It did and it did not help. She changed tack: 'Imagine something beautiful in all the detail you can. Perhaps fir trees, lidded with snow. Or a meadow, with every kind of flower. Try and spot all of the different species, all of their colours, textures and movements. Name them, if you can.' Grace slept.

Tonight, sleep looked unlikely. And she had an early morning. She looked across at Frances, stood by the table. She had one arm bent behind her thin frame, her palm pressing the fabric of her jacket against her back. Her brown hair was cut straight across forming a line of curls under her ears. All the girls wore it that way before, Grace thought, but it seemed a little unusual now. A deliberate gesture backwards, like her golden, embroidered velvet jacket. Grace wondered if she always dressed this way – stood that way, even, with one foot in front of the other in those shoes, or if it was part of the night's machinery. She drank from her cup – the tea was a little cold.

Frances put her cup down and blinked slowly in a movement that raised her eyebrows and stretched her carefully lined eyelids. Grace assumed this meant they were to begin. She gathered the cups, clanking them into a stack as she walked around the table. Kathryn Edwards had left hers neatly, spoon tucked in, but Sam never finished his – always leaving an irritating mulch of water and leaves at the bottom. He joked that any tea or coffee she made him lasted exactly as long as their conversation, but he never finished the damn drinks. She stashed them in a large, intricately painted bowl – intended for trifle, or meringues and cream, but which she used in lieu of a proper sink. While she was busy, Frances had swept the table clean, moving a pile of books, the newspaper and some cigarette ends onto the bed. Grace didn't feel like taking notes. She put the pen and paper on the floor, under the table.

Frances flicked off the lights and sat down at the table, opposite Grace. She left the candle burning in the centre. 'Uncross your legs,' Frances said. Sam chuckled, and kicked at the sole of Grace's foot until she untangled herself. 'This is a sacred circle, Frances explained. 'You must put your name into the circle by saying it aloud.' (They did so.) 'If we are visited, you have to strongly say "yes", "yes" you want to receive this message. And finally, you must say "yes", you want to accept this message. These are two different things.' Frances did her slow and tiresome blink again. She had a grey streak – a single curl – just behind her right ear. 'Are there any other psychics in the room?' Frances asked. Sam looked at Grace, who was staring at the blurred edges of the candle flame.

'I have a message for Sam,' Frances said. It seemed rather quick. 'Sam would you like to receive this message?' 'Yes.' 'There is a handsome young man that knows you from afar,' Frances said. She had switched instantly from the slightly nervous, circuitous patter she made as she drank the tea (irritating in its own way) to these wooden statements (equally irritating, though differently so). Sam stared at her. 'Is that familiar?' asked Frances. 'I'm thinking,' said Sam. 'He says he is enamoured with you.' Did she think he was vain? 'Perhaps we don't know each other properly,' he replied.

Frances explained further, her eyes on the orange light playing on Grace's brooch. 'I told him I wasn't sure who he is. He's giving me a lot of complex, odd images. The most prominent is a gold wedding band spinning inside a walnut. Yes, that one is quite clear. It is a proposal, or maybe just a proposition.' Sam was impassive. 'He's a bit younger than you. He had a very turbulent life. A difficult family life. Is that familiar?' He nodded. 'There's a blue windbreaker, or an overcoat. Does that mean anything?' 'Yes,' said Sam. He picked at his bottom lip with his left hand, pulling it until it pinched. 'Can I leave you with this message?' asked Frances. 'Yes,' said Sam.

Frances's messages were odd, both poetic and superficial. She turned to Kathryn and said, 'I can see hummingbirds spinning out of your hands, a volcano of light beaming out of your forehead.' She was intransigent on peculiar details, such as a beard, but happy to root around various family members until she found the right name or relation. 'I'm getting the name Maureen,' she said, their hour almost up and looking once again at Sam. 'I know several Maureens,' he said. 'Maureen wants you to know that you are keeping her memory alive,' Frances told him. 'All of my Maureens are on this side,' said Sam, showing his front teeth. She put her hands together, and looked as though she was finishing. Kathryn put her pen down and smoothed the pages of the notebook. Then Frances opened her mouth once more. Kathryn picked up her pen. Sam tapped his heel on the floor. Grace pressed her knuckles against her cheekbone. 'I have just received the thought – taken from the Bible. "And I will visit the sins of the fathers unto the children even unto the second and third generation", etc.' Grace tapped the table with her blunt nails. Frances closed the circle with some mutterings and a prayer and it was over. The endings were always sudden, with Frances altering her posture and expressions immediately. Grace switched on the lights. Sam's mouth churned with a muffled yawn. Kathryn was stacking the pages. She handed them over to Grace, who laid them on a side table to type up.

It was late. The guests pulled on their coats, kissed Grace and made their way out into the sticky summer darkness. Grace retrieved the stack of notes. These were reasonably comprehensible, at least, though she would – as she always did – have to work around what was on the page, filling in the gaps and excising sensitive material.

Grace hadn't believed her, until Frances explained that Hart had her write the words her father, Clinton, used to open and close his letters. Frances wrote quickly on a sheet of paper, folded it and placed it in Grace's hand. Grace opened it. It said: 'My Biggest and Best', 'Your oldest Sweetheart'. They had tried other experiments, with Frances receiving written messages, where single words would fill the entire page, wobbly letters guided by the spirit's hand, or whatever it was. These took a great deal of deciphering, guesswork even.

She flicked through the typed pages, finding a record from the previous autumn: 27 October 1940. Another typed note, this time a communication passed from C.A. through Hart. 'Through me, father is sending you his soul's love and all forgiveness and begs you to forgive him. You owe father a debt and he owes you one.' A few days later, the messages were peculiar, relating to fleas. She had added a note, explaining that Hart must have overheard their conversation before establishing the circle. Grace and Frances had watched a flea circus perform, and he began: 'Speaking of fleas', as if he had been sat with them as they drank tea and snapped biscuits.

Grace chewed the inner corner of her cheek and put the papers face down, securing them with a heavy-bottomed glass. There was probably time to wash the cups before she fell asleep. Frances always said this was the best time to hear something, in that space between sleeping and waking. She waited in bed, listening.

15

Lovers

Among the set of portraits Walker Evans made of Hart Crane is a silver-cast photograph of Hart's hands. One curls into a gentle fist, the other just about holds it, nails bitten to nothing. Evans knew how significant hands were to Hart's writing. In Hart's poems, love is expressed by erotic unions or it is yearning, present in absence.

In his poetic universe, quiet contentment between lovers is rare – love is 'piracy', Hart writes. Bodies rock, 'flung from dawn to dawn', they mingle 'mutual blood'. There is the occasional quiet image: a face buried in 'bright hair', 'eyes already sealed', dreaming of 'the slant of drifting foam' as a sailor lover sleeps. Or a memory intrudes while he rides the subway: 'And why do I often meet your visage here, / Your eyes like agate lanterns – on and on'. Images of touching and not touching haunt the poems. Muscles tense – 'spry cordage' – with anticipation. Hands meet or don't and helplessly reach out: 'There is some way, I think, to touch / Those hands of yours that count the night', says Hart's Faustus to Helen. 'Permit me voyage, love, into your hands . . .' he says to one of the many lovers that feature in 'Voyages'. And these silent communications often fail: a man walks along Bleecker Street 'Wounded by apprehensions out of speech', by unspoken forms of language.

At nineteen, I loved these poems and their intense, violent images, which offered me a way of articulating my own desires: for the boy counting derelict buildings for his geography project; the spit of Peter Fonda first glimpsed across a wide, busy street; sat in the kitchen of my student halls on my first night, too tall for the booth; bright green eyes, running up the lecture-theatre stairs in a leather jacket and big, laced boots.

A biography tells us as much about the writer as its subject. Love and desire work in a similar way – both require that we construct our own version of another person. If we appear to fall in love at first sight, perhaps we are falling in love with a projection of ourselves: what we want that person to be (we cannot know it), which might tell us what we want to be. Desire – in its many forms – can tell us a great deal about ourselves. I have found ambition to be sublimated into erotic desire. A form of displacement: I cannot admit that he possesses a quality I want to possess, so I want him, admiring that quality instead of cultivating it in myself. This doesn't mean that it's not real, but that it gives us information about ourselves beyond sexual attraction.

The narratives we traditionally associate with women use love and parenthood as key structuring principles – the denouement, even, whereafter she disappears. They have been kicked against for a long time, but these structures are resilient. In Greta Gerwig's version of *Little Women*, Jo, who is writing a book, cries to her mother in their attic and says: 'I'm so sick of people saying that love is just all a woman is fit for' – a refor-mulation of a speech made in Louisa May Alcott's novel a good 150 years before. Erotic desire is embarrassing, but not as embarrassing as ambition – as Jo knows, making her speech anyway, her cheeks red hot – declaring that you want to be a writer or an artist, that you want to be scalding, brilliant.

In her essay 'Uses of the Erotic', Audre Lorde wrote that the erotic is one of many kinds of power, 'used and unused, acknowledged or otherwise.' 'For women', she writes, 'this has meant a suppression of the erotic as a considered source of power and information within our lives.' It is a knowledge wrenched from within, Lorde explains, that we therefore mistrust; but, if acknowledged and considered, might give us the tools to nurture joy, 'whether physical, emotional, psychic, or intellectual', in turn forming bridges between individuals. Eroticism is feared, Lorde writes, because once we begin to feel deeply, we start to demand more, to demand 'that joy which we know ourselves to be capable of', living from within in a manner that demands total responsibility for oneself – pursu-ing joy, whether it be artistic, intellectual, physical, emotional.

Looking at Hart through the eyes of his lovers tells us some-thing about him. We see his most awful aspects: Hart seen through a glass darkly, his jealousies, defensiveness, manipula-tions. But we can also glimpse his joyous capacity for love. In Mexico, Hart had many lovers that we know nothing about, aside from glimpses in his writing of their bathing together in 'mountain streams'. The occasional detail in letters to his friend Solomon Grunberg survive. An amateur psychoanalyst with a reductive knowledge of Freud, he was dangerous for Hart. He was a friend with whom Hart was relatively open, and who also seemed determined to persuade Hart away from homosexuality. In 1966, he outlined his armchair analysis of Hart for Unterecker: 'He was not a homosexual in the accepted sense of the term. That type of homosexuality that he suffered from – not that he enjoyed – was nothing but a compulsion, neurosis, and to that degree I go with Freud. He had no use for inverts . . .' He described Hart's letters, claiming that he was scathing of any hint of effeminacy in other gay men: 'That's when I read the word "f--". He called them "f---".'

It is unclear if Grunberg's depiction of Hart was entirely accurate, or if Hart's prejudices fluctuated depending on his mood or audience. For instance, describing an exciting affair with a pilot in California, he wrote to William Slater Brown that 'I never could stand much falsetto, you know'. Meanwhile, he told Bill Wright, virtually on the same day, of his fascination with the 'little fairies' on Hollywood Boulevard. Sam, whose own poetry collection *The Hermaphrodite* worried at gender binaries, explained that Hart seemed to have a fraught view of masculinity. He seemed to have 'schooled' himself to appear masculine, so that he 'could not tolerate feminine people' of any gender. Hart wrote of Grace that 'I think my mother has something of the lesbian in her. She's very cold.' While he had women friends, he did not always take women seriously, particularly when they criticised his poetry. He characterised the women editors of *Poetry* (Harriet Monroe) and *The Dial* (Marianne Moore) as 'hysterical virgins'. Hart, who was scolded by his aunt for playing with his mother's dresses and trimming her hats, was made 'nervous' by deviations from what he considered to be masculine.

And was it any wonder that he retained this nervousness into adulthood, when friends such as Porter could not mask their own prejudices. In June, Porter wrote a letter to Hart striking at what she perceived as his femininity; she interprets his apparent difficulty regulating his mood as 'emotional hysteria' with a 'taste for melodrama', foreshadowing her later comments on his 'twin vices' (as she saw it: homosexuality and alcohol). This was familiar. Contemporary reviews of Hart's poetry were stuffed with sly, derisory allusions to his sexuality. His poetry was 'vapid', they said. It lacked 'discipline' and reason. It was yielding, it was fluid, unmoored.

One review, written by the influential literary critic and activist Max Eastman, and an acquaintance of Hart's from Greenwich Village, constructed a metaphor for Hart's poems. He imagined them as a woman's mouth, her lips painted red and waiting not to speak but to receive. *The Bridge*, figured as a mouth, Eastman explained, 'gazes out of the page significantly and in my direction but will not open its lips, will not make friends – will not, as we say "come out with it."' Anita Brenner was so outraged that she wrote a response, an unpublished essay called 'Give to Caesar', in which she took the central image and recast it as a shrill feminine scream. 'No hables de lo que no entiendes', she wrote back to Eastman ('Don't talk about what you don't understand').

In October 1931, Hart wrote to Grunberg discussing his sexual encounters with Mexican men. 'I wish I could tell you something about my travels into the country . . . but that would take a book, so would my sex life down here.' Shortly after, hoping to please his friend, he wrote again, explaining he was in love with a woman, Peggy Cowley, a landscape painter and the estranged wife of his friend Malcolm. The relationship, coming close on the heels of his father's death, was a 'great consolation to a loneliness that had about eaten me up', as Hart told Sam.

Peggy had arrived in Mexico City in late June, shortly before Hart left for Ohio. She was unwell, struggling with her recent separation and beginning the divorce process. Born Marguerite Frances Baird in 1890, Peggy's paintings and writings have been lost to posterity. When she is mentioned (precisely as I am doing here), it is because of her relationships with famous men: the poet Orrick Johns, Malcolm Cowley, the playwright Eugene O'Neill and, of course, Hart Crane.

According to Matthew Josephson, a writer and a close mutual friend of Peggy and Hart, she 'liked to live in charming disorder'. If she borrowed ten dollars for food, she would spend the majority on flowers. She was not attached to monogamy. She loved all-night poker games and hated washing up. She was tiny and thin with reddish hair. Her eyes were the colour of brandy. This strange combination gave her a magical, elfin quality.

Like Hart, Peggy was a fixture in the Village in the 1910s. She smoked and drank a great deal. She loved cats and flowers. Peggy was a suffragist. In 1917 she joined the National Woman's Party, alongside her dear friend and comrade, Dorothy Day, the journalist, social activist and anarchist. In November the group picketed the White House and obstructed traffic, for which they were imprisoned. The protestors were kept in the Occoquan Workhouse in Virginia for two weeks, where she went on hunger strike. She stared at the top of her bunk, wrote poetry and sketched. Their arrest was eventually deemed unlawful and the group was released. Two years later, she and her first husband Orrick Johns divorced. The same year, 1919, she met Malcolm Cowley and they married. He had just returned from the war in France, where he was in the Ambulance Corps. She wanted children but could not have them.

Peggy's friends describe her as forgiving (particularly, according to Susan Jenkins Brown, when it came to alcoholic tantrums) and 'an undemanding dependent, rather like a well-disposed child.' This idea of her dependency was perhaps the result of her affairs, where she is seen as an adjunct to male genius, utterly ignoring her youthful involvement with the suffragists. Perhaps her talents might have matched theirs, but evidence of any brilliance has all but vanished, aside from the odd beautifully constructed letter or moment in her memoir of Hart.

When Hart returned, Peggy was staying with Katherine Anne Porter while she looked for her own place and waited for her divorce to become final. Hart was sure that Peggy would have heard awful stories from Porter. But she was keen to see him. Because of Hart's closeness to Malcolm Cowley and their circle in New York, 'Hart represented to me the family life I had just lost', she explained, 'making me no longer an exile. And he felt much the same way about me. We were "home" to each other, and both of us needed "home."' Peggy was often sick, and Hart would nurse her with dry crackers and water. He visited her after his trips to flea markets, tipping the contents of his bag about her room, with serapes of 'wonderful color, weave and design', glass ornaments and kitchenware, figures sculpted from clay, armfuls of flowers.

Hart planned a trip to Taxco, bringing Peggy with him to meet Spratling. 'She's pretty fragile', Hart told him, 'but I think she's happy here.' Aged seventy-six, Peggy recalled how Hart made her laugh as they wandered around Taxco. ' "Facts" were unimportant in his life', wrote Peggy, 'and if confronted with such balderdash he would instantly roar it away.' By November, his Spanish had made little progress, Peggy observed. It was 'a hodge-podge of words strung together with gestures – an animated picture with sound.' 'He was a great great person, even if he did drag the nerves out by the roots at times, he could also be a sweetheart,' she said.

As they walked through Mexico City, often accompanied by Lesley Simpson, Hart would invent backstories for people passing by in the streets. The average stranger might be a pimp, a cut-throat, a prostitute, a femme fatale or a prince. A man's jaw became a bold line on a canvas by Leonardo da Vinci under his gaze. A housewife, shopping bag under her arm stuffed with vegetables, was up to no good, 'a typical tart from the word go'.

In November, something in their friendship began to shift. It began inauspiciously. After one confusing night with Peggy, which had ended with the two hurling insults at each other, Hart wrote her a letter outlining a scene: 'If you wanted to go farther, as you claimed, last night – how could you expect me to, with Maria sick on the bed, and the floor covered with vomit!' It is unclear who the sick Maria was, but it seems sensible to assume it was Peggy's housekeeper, Maria Louisa. He followed it up with another note: 'I don't think you need bother to consider me a friend anymore', then attempted to visit the house with Daniel – they were refused entry.

Vomit aside, the two became inseparable. But Peggy was still unwell. Fearing the city's altitude was not helping her lungs, Hart suggested she move out to Taxco until February. Peggy needed to be somewhere warm, among friends. She took a house owned by Natalie Scott, a writer, journalist, translator and former Red Cross nurse in Siqueiros's and Brum's circle. Peggy took a long, terrifying bus ride down to Taxco. Spratling met her when she arrived and took her to the new house, close enough to his that they could call to each other over a ravine.

The house, as Peggy described it, was 'a tiny white spot on the top of an inaccessible mountain, with steps cut into the ascent.' 'Only a goat can climb that,' she thought. When she arrived at the top, she loved it. It had panoramic views of the town and countryside and came with two dogs and a pair of egrets that made love constantly. Hart nicknamed the birds Gretchen and Charles, though he 'could never distinguish one from the other, except at certain critical moments in their dialogue.'

Telegrams from Hart arrived immediately, forcing messengers to run up and down the steep steps to the house. Peggy planned a party over Christmas, inviting her eclectic group of artist, poet and painter friends. Hart arrived early, while Peggy was in the bath. She threw on clothes and rushed from the veranda and down the steep steps into his arms. 'He dropped the suitcase and we embraced as if it had been years since we had seen each other,' Peggy wrote. Maria Louisa, and her gardener, Jesús, were watching. Peggy didn't bother to explain that they weren't together, 'he wasn't "mine" in their sense of the word.'

Peggy called over the ravine to Spratling, inviting him to join them. She made drinks: rum with fresh lime squeezed into the glass. Spratling arrived with a Christmas gift: silver earrings shaped like baskets full of flowers. Peggy put them on straight away, choosing a dress to match. Later, she remembered Hart twirling her around after she had changed, the fabric spinning. He stepped back, 'Isn't she wonderful, Bill? I'll fall in love with you,' he told her. 'Of course, I really am already.' They slept apart that night. Hart, silver-haired and laughing, brought her orange juice and coffee, a cigar in one hand making broad circles of smoke and full of plans to decorate the house. 'Mexico is wrapped in tinsel,' Hart said. He covered the house in red and green, poinsettias everywhere – two hundred, Peggy claimed – and 'twenty-five strange yellow blooms'.

A dozen other guests arrived on Christmas Eve. Peggy's crowd included Hart, the painter Clinton King, Lady Duff Twysden ('Brett' in Hemingway's *The Sun Also Rises*), and the poet Witter Bynner. They drank, shouted lewd limericks into the night from Peggy's windows and balcony and eventually staggered into Midnight Mass in the cathedral, where there was beautiful singing. The crowd emptied out after Christmas Day, and Hart and Peggy spent a week alone.

The plan was to work hard during the rest of Hart's stay: he would sit at his typewriter, she at hers. No more drinking and parties, they promised each other over lunch, having seen off the guests. They climbed their way up to the house, sober.

Back in their 'eagle's nest', bells started to ring. Fireworks zinged and skidded through the skies. 'It can't last!' Hart shouted over the dinner table. The noise continued. They might as well join the dancing down in the plaza. They danced until they were exhausted, 'everything appeared to be spinning', wrote Peggy, 'off into an infinity of color and music.'

That night, they both slept in Peggy's bed, 'the clamor of the bells our wedding music', she wrote. The next morning, Maria Louisa brought coffee and orange juice. 'She had never done this before. Somehow it showed us she put an official seal on our union.' Hart seemed excited, Peggy wrote. 'He kept looking at me and laughing.' She was 'Twidget', he was 'Mizzentrop'.

He was writing again, perhaps thanks to his routine with Peggy, with the two sitting down to work for a few hours each day. During this heady period, he began work on a new poem, 'The Broken Tower'. He started, as was his habit, with sketches, before working through full drafts of the poem in late January and early February. In acute, beautiful prose that suggests the brilliance with which she might have tackled her own ideas, Peggy recalled Hart's working process and confusions. The bells 'seemed to clarify his thought', she explained, his phonograph blaring. Peggy wrote that:

> Teasing, I asked if he thought he could concentrate on writing the poem. And so he began, phrases scribbled on paper, voiced in words to test the sound, discarded completely, or held for a later trial. He was the instrument on which he played the words, changing each perhaps a hundred times before retaining one small fragment.

The poem, which rings with the sounds of the bells from that Christmas night, is in part an epithalamion for his unofficial bride, in part a meditation on his past affairs. Hart writes in 'The Broken Tower':

> And so it was I entered the broken world
> To trace the visionary company of love, its voice,
> An instant on the wind (I know not wither hurled)
> But not for long to hold each desperate choice.

Again, love is something that is traced and fleeting. A lover, here, is one of many desperate choices. He asks himself: 'My word I poured. But was it cognate', by which he means is this love poem the same as he had written before with doomed excitement or, worse perhaps, was it even in his voice? Was it 'cognate', meaning somehow derivative, borrowed from another poet. There were no simple explanations for what he was experiencing, even 'my blood left me / No answer', he writes. What can be relied upon, he decides, is the joyous spinning and complexity of language. That is a 'bell-rope' to swing upon, in all directions.

When they were apart, he wrote her constant letters and notes: 'I missed your darling hands last night.' They drank too much, smoked too much, argued, and lay in bed in Mixcoac and out in Taxco. The opacity of Hart's letters to Peggy and about Peggy are both crude and beautiful. He wrote numerous letters to friends, including Sam, boasting about the 'bed springs' that might be heard throughout Mexico City. But there is something melancholy in them, read against other letters to his friends, which communicate his love for Emil Opffer through metaphors and knowing omissions. No letters to Emil survive. What is known about their relationship comes from the recollections of mutual friends and the odd comment from Emil.

Hart and Emil met in 1923, introduced through Susan Jenkins Brown. Emil was two years Hart's senior, one of four Danish brothers, all blond and blue-eyed. According to Sam, he was 'yellow and stocky, nice wholesome looking'. He would turn up at the Browns unexpectedly, 'loaded down with large bags containing Scandinavian delicacies, bottles of wine protruding', and proceed to lay out a Danish smorgasbord for all present.' Emil was excitable, boyish and stubborn. Hart adored him. Susan Jenkins Brown explained that, one night, Emil had arrived at her house in 'a most depressed state'. Hart set about trying to cheer him up. 'They made a night of it, and Emil was soon overwhelmed by the devotion of that tornado.'

Emil went to sea. Hart wrote him long letters. In April 1924, Emil walked through New York. He called Susan and got Hart's address. Later, he remembered: 'Find the house. Knock on the door, Hart writing with the radio going, and stayed all night with him on the narrow bed.' Hart nicknamed him 'Goldilocks.' Hart told Sam that he loved Emil desperately. A few days later, Hart arrived outside Emil's lodging and shouted to him from the street, declaring that he loved him. Emil had to move out. Hart took an apartment at 110 Columbia Heights, in the same building as Emil's father and on the same road as Sam. Hart and Emil could practically live together, seeing each other under the cover of Emil's visits to his father. When he wanted to stay longer, he borrowed the novelist John Dos Passos's apartment, also on Columbia Heights.

The apartment overlooked Manhattan. 'Just imagine', Hart told Grace, 'looking out your window on the East River with nothing intervening between your view of the Statue of Liberty, way down the harbor, and the marvelous beauty of Brooklyn Bridge close above you on your right!' Later, Hart would move to a different room in the building, previously inhabited by John Augustus Roebling, the architect of the bridge. When Roebling was dying, he had a telescope set up to watch the construction of his masterpiece.

Hart was writing copy for *Sweet's Catalog*, which sold building products. While he was working in the office, Hart snuck in time for his own writing, turning his notes for the first of the six 'Voyages' into poems, when he should have been producing advertisements. At lunchtime, Emil would occasionally meet him and his friends – Matthew Josephson, Malcolm Cowley,

William Slater Brown – for coffee and cinnamon toast at the Brazilian Coffee House on West 43rd Street.

Emil was one of many sailors. Sam tells a story that, through another Scandinavian, Hart had access to a boat on the Hudson. Hart would sometimes invite a few of his sailor friends up there. 'I leave the rest up to your imagination,' Sam explained in an interview with Unterecker. The Scandinavian would cruise around, and Hart enjoyed the ready supply of alcohol and the ebb and flow of men through the day. Sam arrived one afternoon, and there was Hart sat on the bed reading from *The Bridge* or *Moby Dick* – he couldn't remember. In front of him was a stoker, thick-set and with fingers blackened from the coal. Hart greeted Sam with a 'hello' and continued reading.

Although Hart was unable to be direct in his letters, it was the necessary circumnavigations around his sexual and romantic experiences that produced the stunning movements of 'Voyages'. In his poem 'Voyages IV' Hart describes waiting for Emil at sea, imagining his lover counting 'hours and days' through the 'spectrum of sea', time passing as the waves and horizon shifted as Emil approached New York. The poem is stuffed with phrases first thought out in Hart's letters to friends, in which he tried to hint at their relationship. In a letter to Waldo Frank, Hart described Emil in biblical terms as the 'word made flesh' ('and the word was made flesh', John 1:14), suggesting Emil is love or eroticism incarnate – the absolute ideal of what Hart desired. His Adam – the beginning and the end of his desires. But he is also suggesting that Emil is at the heart of his poetry – his 'signature'. That his poetry will be energised and find its forms through his attempts to write about the man that he loves: physical acts made abstract, written down.

Hart forged a connection between the poem and the physical body in his work. When he writes of 'New thresholds, new
anatomies' in the poem 'The Wine Menagerie', he is describing
his attempts to document his relationships, and the new forms
of language that he was forced to develop, given that he could
not write openly about his affairs with men without risking
censorship. Even *The Bridge* can be seen this way, a grand land-
mark and image of connection that was also the view from his
and Emil's bedroom.

These attempts to create moments of intimacy in his poems
extended beyond Hart's friends, lovers – even his parents – and
to the writers that came before him. The writer and theorist
Lauren Berlant wrote that intimacy is 'portable, unattached to
a concrete space'. In other words, it can be forged through the
imagination, conversation, by writing – proximity is not neces-
sarily required. So many poets have understood this, and have
written to and about Hart: Eileen Myles, John Berryman,
Robert Lowell, Frank O'Hara, Allen Ginsberg, Adrienne Rich,
Robert Creeley, Mark Ford, Orlando Ricardo Menes, Geoffrey
Hill, John Wieners, Hunce Voelcker, and, as it happens, my
own boyfriend, whose elegy to Hart Crane winged its way to
my computer screen one January morning. The poet Alfred
Corn put it this way:

The truth may lie in imagining a connection
With him or with you; with anyone able to overlook
Distance, shrug off time, on the right occasion . . .

Hart believed in shrugging off time, in friendships and
connections with writers long dead. In the 'Cape Hatteras'
section of *The Bridge* (first published in Paris, illustrated by

Evans's photographs of Brooklyn Bridge), Hart imagines himself palm to palm with that great nineteenth-century poet and lover of 'adhesive males' and 'comradeship', Walt Whitman. In 'Whoever you are holding me now in hand', Whitman addresses the queer writers that might follow him, borrowing the erotic codes of his poems for their own. There is, he suggests, an eroticism in unpicking these coded images. *Leaves of Grass* transforms into a medium for sexual communion across generations:

> Or if you will, thrusting me beneath your clothing,
> Where I may feel the throbs of your heart or rest upon
> your hip,
> Carry me when you go forth over land or sea;
> For thus touching you would I silently sleep and be
> carried eternally.

Hart carried these lines with him: 'in the slant of the drifting foam . . . Draw in your head and sleep the long way home.' His poetry stays close to Whitman's, borrowing his tricks.

Like Whitman, the landscape could be transformed, turning into a proxy for the poet's touch. In Whitman's 'Song of Myself', a young woman with 'Twenty-eight years of womanly life and all so lonesome' watches through the window as 'Twenty-eight young men bathe by the shore'. Whitman looks at her looking at the men on the beach. Their beards are glistening wet and water runs from 'long hair' in streams. In a moment of fantasy, she watches from the window and sees herself stepping out onto the beach. An 'unseen hand' passes over the bathers' bodies. It descends, 'trembling from their temples and ribs'.

Appearing and disappearing, it is both the touch of the young woman and the poet as the two combine. In another transformation, she and he seem to melt into the sea as 'The young men float on their backs', held by the 'puff and declines' of the waves with each 'pendant and bending arch'. Hart borrows this in 'Voyages': 'The sea lifts, also, reliquary hands', he tells a lover, a sailor, 'your body rocking!'.

In the final lines of the 'Cape Hatteras' section of *The Bridge*, Hart addresses Whitman in a gesture of friendship that reaches back into the previous century, ending with a suggestive silence. 'My hand / in yours, / Walt Whitman – ' he writes, 'so – '.

Traditionally, a practice called handfasting could be performed as an unofficiated marriage or betrothal. As a verb *handfast* is derived from the Old Norse: to strike a bargain by joining hands. In Middle English, the action transformed slightly to mean to formally promise or to make a contract. A handfasting ceremony could be performed anywhere, the couple simply needed to take each other's right hand, declaring their marriage. Like Shakespeare's holy palmer's kiss, for Hart the touching of hands is at once serious and erotic: 'your hands within my hands are deeds', he writes, 'my tongue upon your throat, singing'. A 'deed' is both an intentional action and a signed legal document. In his poems we find a series of fleeting marriages that are no less significant for their brevity.

Hart wrote a poem dedicated to Emil, 'The Visible the Untrue'. Hart describes 'fingernails that cinch' in a tight grasp as he waits for the 'unkind farewell' of Emil's inevitable departure to sea. The poem ('To E.O.') also seems be an apology for his erratic behaviour. Hart describes himself as 'the terrible puppet of my dreams', acting unthinkingly, perhaps in the service of jealousy. Emil found Hart 'impossible when drunk'.

He rambled incessantly and they quarrelled. One night, he sat waiting for Hart in a Russian tearoom. Hart arrived and, according to Emil, 'came marching in across the hushed floor like a madman, stood glowering and masculine, pointing his finger, & cried – "You whore!" and marched out.' In reality, Hart and Emil had both continued to take lovers, even while they were together. William Slater Brown indicated that there were constant 'betrayals' on both sides. Sam's recollection was that the relationship ended when Emil caught Hart with another man at 110 Columbia Heights. Emil eventually married, settling in Copenhagen.

Peggy and Hart planned a honeymoon of sorts after the discovery of their relationship in Taxco. Hart returned to Mexico City on 5 January. He had a little money, with advances arranged by Bess. He sent Peggy seventy-five dollars when he got home and wrote: 'I'm in such a hectic rush ... dying now to be off to Acapulco with you in two weeks' time, almost every morning must be bent to that end ... I can't do more than remind you that you already know the depth of my love to you.' 'The ride home', he explained, was 'psychologically so strange and new a meditation to me that it seemed almost like sheer delirium.'

When Hart was away, Peggy enjoyed the quiet. She sat on the veranda with coffee and a cigarette, looking at the sun brushing the mountains 'honeycombed with abandoned silver mines'. From her perch she could hear the gentle sounds of the town rising up to the house: the odd voice and clatter, musical instruments, church bells.

Back in Mixcoac, Hart wrote a flurry of letters. It felt like 'beginning all over again', Hart told Grunberg. It was his first sexual experience with a woman – 'the newest adventure I ever had.' He returned to Peggy soon, arriving on 18 January for the town's saint's name day, Santa Prisca, a young martyr, sacrificed by the Emperor Claudius to Apollo. Hart appeared as Peggy was on the veranda, a clang of bells starting up once again. They whirled around town, finding the tail end of a procession. Each person in the procession carried or led a gilded animal: horses with golden hooves, a green pig on a purple ribbon, a white cat with blotches of pink on its fur. There were green parrots dyed blue and vice versa. A cockatiel with a silver cast. A turkey with a necklace of Christmas beads. A bull tried to mount a passing cow in the melee. A priest stood to one side, blessing each member of the parade as they walked by.

After the festivities, the two dragged themselves back up the cut steps and discussed their plans: perhaps Acapulco, but Hart was increasingly concerned about money. A letter from Bess had arrived, explaining the reality of his financial situation. There was nothing. His mood slipped the following day and he went into town. He couldn't stop drinking and landed in jail. Peggy was furious. She called Spratling, who headed down to the station. He would have to stay there for the night and sleep it off, Spratling reported, passing on a message: 'Hart thinks you are acting high hat.' He never apologised. 'They were affronts to his dignity,' Peggy wrote. 'It never entered his head that I was in any way affected. That I was already in an unconventional position, made no pleasanter by notoriety.'

Their first argument had occurred some weeks before their sexual relationship began, with Lesley Simpson as a witness. One night in November, Hart had emerged from a taxi, 'having a fuss with a taxi driver and the porter', accusing him of hiking up his fare. According to Simpson, the scene was a 'riot'. Hart was dressed offensively (though he did not deem it so). Peggy recorded his outfit as 'a costume that I'm sure he thought of as that of a Mexican gentleman'. The 'costume' was an arrangement of white flannel trousers, a brown and white serape and a large, jauntily perched straw sombrero tied with a multi-coloured cord. Around his neck he wore the silver bridle. Dressed as he was, a trophy of colonisation coupled with native dress, Hart expected his Indigenous servant, Daniel, to wait on him and appease the taxi drivers. Peggy and Lesley did not take Hart's side. The whole scene was an insult. She and Lesley were tired of being his diplomats.

Their arguments continued. Hart's earliest model for a romantic relationship was that of his parents, before their eventual divorce, characterised by patterns of estrangement and reunion. They quarrelled. Grace or C.A. would leave the family home, followed by 'violent sexual reconciliations' – Waldo Frank's words, not Hart's, recalling a conversation he had with Hart in Paris. Grace's use of silence, blocking out C.A. when they argued, was a weapon that she also aimed at her son. His letters are full of references to this: 'Well, after two months of absolute silence, I'm glad to hear from you.' Hart appears to have done the same, his letters to Peggy suggesting similar patterns: 'I was in the mood for swearing last night that I wouldn't write you for at least a week', he told her shortly after Valentine's Day. He was, at least, reflective, explaining that he had hoped 'a long glum silence' would worry her.

He could be the same with friends, as his behaviour with Porter made clear. Sam recalled two arguments with Hart during their friendship. The first began with a disagreement over poetry, as Hart criticised the work of a late mutual friend,

Ernest W. Nelson, to whom Hart wrote an elegy in 1922, 'Praise for an Urn'. The two fought until Sam left Hart's apartment. Hart picked it up again the next day, writing Sam an angry note. They didn't speak for six months. The next: Hart came up to Sam's apartment at Columbia Heights. He drank too much and tried to smash things. Sam prised him out of the door. Hart stood outside, hammering. Eventually he went downstairs, and banged his own door open and shut all night long. The next morning, Sam went downstairs to confront him. Hart didn't remember a thing. 'I'm not your nursemaid,' Sam told him. He looked pitiful. Sam kissed his forehead and shook his hand – that was the end of it.

Hart's drinking worsened, as he admitted in letters to his stepmother. Those who suffer from it describe alcoholism as a progressive disease. There is a belief that, even if you are thirty years sober, the progression has still continued, so that if you picked up a bottle that would be it. You would be as deep in it as if you had drunk all those years. Susan Jenkins Brown believed this, writing that 'in his last year or so a resumption of drinking would, within a few hours, reduce him to the lowest level that he had previously reached and then plunge him even lower.' There are traces of Hart's desperation among his declarations of happiness. Peggy was 'something of a reason for living', he wrote. 'Why is it you love me so?', Hart asked her shortly after his return to the city. 'I don't deserve it. I'm just a careening idiot, with a talent for humor at times, and for insult and desecration at others.' His mood was erratic, plummeting before rising once more. Peggy wrote:

> I was as necessary as the bells which seemed to clarify his thought. His energy seemed inexhaustible. He was keyed

to the highest pitch. Yet this experience was somewhat frightening to him. I, too, was more than a little disturbed. He had confided to me that for some time he had feared that he would never again feel the urge to write, and now he was again writing poetry. He had found something beyond sensuality, he felt purified of a sense of guilt which he had always had as a homosexual.

Hart planned to sublet his house in Mixcoac, but was unable to find a tenant. He gave up, and made do with travelling backwards and forwards to Taxco, until Peggy moved into his house in February. Hart was anxious about money, and that Peggy might expect too much of him romantically. He was fearful that they might 'urge the other into anything but the most spontaneous and liberal arrangements', but reassured her that they were 'bound' more than he had 'ever dreamed of being, and in the most pleasant and deep way.'

And yet he also needed her close. Peggy's version is that Hart started a 'campaign' to get her to move, centred on Hart's fights with Daniel. Hart claimed he needed Peggy to intervene in their chaotic relationship – a friendship clouded by their master–servant relationship and Hart's clear insensitivities. Peggy describes Daniel as 'harried' and harassed by Hart's temper. Hart was growing paranoid. Both of Daniel's brothers were policemen, who had likely helped Hart evade trouble. But it increasingly became a source of delusion. Lisa, Hart's live-in friend, was convinced Daniel would shop her to the police 'on account of her political affiliations'. Peggy was sceptical. She liked Daniel, and didn't believe that he was drunkenly threatening Hart with knives and revolvers. In any case, she thought, it would all quieten down if she moved in.

When Peggy arrived from Taxco, Hart met her at their favourite restaurant in town, Broadway. Hart appeared in a white linen suit with a corsage of orchids. As they entered, cocktails miraculously appeared, and the table was decked out with her favourite flowers: sweet peas. Daniel was behaving, Hart said, he had been 'sweeping like a mad Dutch housewife' and was out and about gathering flowers to decorate the house for Peggy's arrival. That night, they ate and caught a Charlie Chaplin film in a theatre stinking of piss, laughing until they both cried.

At home in Mixcoac, the house was immaculate. There were flowers and sheaves of wheat in vases in each room. The Siqueiros portrait loomed from a wall in Hart's sparsely decorated bedroom. A kid Hart bought for Peggy skittered around the house, its hooves beating on the tiles. In March, the painter Marsden Hartley arrived, a friend of Hart's from the Village. Mary Louis Doherty, Carleton and Betty Beals, and Lesley Simpson and his wife Marian Hahn visited regularly for coffee and drinks. Marian found him charming, 'a grey-haired youth, gulping chocolate ice cream and soda'.

Peggy wore an onyx ring and a sun hat that Hart had bought her. She picked violets from the garden, trampling Hart's beloved forget-me-nots quite barbarously. They drank two gallons of beer a day. She was exhausted by the altitude and Hart's frenetic activities. She climbed onto the roof of the house, covered with vines and blossoms, to sleep in the sun, day after day. Or she made a nest for them both on the porch, with pillows propping their backs against the stone. He looked like the Siqueiros portrait sat like this, Peggy thought. She wanted to move back to Taxco. She wanted Hart to be her husband, it is unclear if he wanted the same.

But circumstances were pressing in on Hart – 31 March was the last day of his Guggenheim Fellowship. Bess wrote again, explaining that a lawsuit against the Crane Company meant no more advances could be made. Sections of his father's businesses began to declare bankruptcy. Hart would need to cut his cloth. There were 'feverish weeks running hither and thither and yon every day to borrow enough money to keep us going', he told Grunberg. Despite his circumstances, he felt recovery was possible: 'If I can avoid drinking too much I'm expecting to get nearer solid earth than I have for several years', he wrote.

Hart had sent out his new poem to friends and magazines and received no response, not even from Malcolm (in fact his letter was stuck in the post). 'He became ugly', Peggy wrote. The combination of the lack of comment on his new poem, his financial insecurities and his increasing drinking was turning his mind. He began to doubt his ability as a poet, that he had ever written anything of merit. He muttered to himself that he was 'a rat in a trap'. He was sick in the mind and body, shouting tirelessly at Daniel, who was at the time in and out of employment with Hart and a nearby general. Hart threatened to set Peggy 'free' while seeming fearful that she might accept. His sense of what was and what was not real was slipping. When he was jailed, he blamed it on a conspiracy to ruin his reputation. He refused to see acquaintances, and Simpson, who could handle Hart in these moments, was out of town. Hart started to find Peggy irritating. She reminded him of his mother. He liked women to be nuisances, until they started to nuisance him.

One Sunday 17 April, Hart was already drunk by the time Peggy got up. Mary Doherty and another friend, Louise, had arrived at the house, planning a dinner with Peggy. Hart was ranting to himself. His speech was nonsensical, words strung together. There did not seem to be an object for his rage. Mary, Louise and Peggy observed him, waiting. His eyes settled on his portrait. 'The paint is already cracking, it's a daub executed with house paint!' he said. 'What a travesty! Do you think that jackal will be known ten years after he dies?' he said of Siqueiros, and perhaps of himself. He'd be a laughing stock if he took it home, 'gulled into buying that piece of junk'.

He took out his father's razor. Peggy ran towards him. He reached up and forward and sliced across his own eyes, right through the canvas. He put the razor into his pocket and walked into the front room. Daniel had disappeared. What happened next is unverified. As Peggy has it, Hart sat at his desk scribbling on a page. 'It is my last will,' he told the three women. 'Peggy is the only person with faith in me and my ability as a poet', which was, of course, untrue. 'This afternoon I am going to kill myself,' he explained. He paced for hours, drinking liquor. At some point that day he found a bottle of iodine. In front of the three women, he removed the cap and drew it to his mouth. Peggy, Mary and Louise wrestled it off him, the chemical leaving purple marks on his lips and serape.

Daniel reappeared, a doctor in tow. Hart was given a sedative. Mary was concerned about Hart's legal situation, fearing he could be prosecuted for making an attempt on his own life. Peggy nursed him through the night, offering him sips of water and cooling his forehead. He managed to eat a little in the morning. He tried to brush it off – it was too much tequila, he told her. But he was shaken enough to agree to return to the United States.

Peggy went to the bank to wire home for money. After some confusion over the tender, she received her wire from the head of the Bank of Mexico. Across the desk, sat Plutarco Calles, *el Jefe Máximo* – the ex-president, but still essentially in power. His eyes were black and shiny, she recalled. He smiled and passed her the necessary papers in silence. She stammered a response and made her way to the Ward Line to buy tickets for their passage home.

Jobs done, she met with Carleton and Betty Beals for a drink in town, before the three made their way out to the Mixcoac house. In Peggy's absence, Hart had lost the run of himself once again. He wasn't at home. He was sure that Peggy had been robbed, raped, left for dead, something. She had fallen somewhere in the street, alone. He ran into the city to report her disappearance to the police, even heading to the American Embassy to broadcast a notice with her description. He returned, his relief transformed into fury that she was late. He needed rest, Peggy thought. The next morning they finished their packing and dispatched their trunks to the ship.

On their last afternoon in Mexico City, they held a party at the Broadway restaurant for their friends. Hart forced himself into gaiety for the occasion, appearing in good humour. According to Peggy, they announced their engagement. At this point, Peggy had not yet received her divorce papers from Malcolm. Hearing Peggy's claims of their engagement after Hart's death, his friends were sceptical of the plan, doubting his commitment to marriage to a woman. Hart's own letters contain no suggestion that the two were engaged, or were as conventionally coupled as Peggy's account suggests. In fact, while Hart revels in his love for Peggy, he takes pains to emphasise that while he might have 'broken ranks with my much advertised "brotherhood"', the 'old beauty still claims me, however, and my eyes roam as much as ever. I doubt if I'll ever change very fundamentally.' While the two were enjoying a 'conjugal life', it was – in Hart's own words – 'unofficial', with Hart taking lovers. The theorist and writer Eve Kosofsky Sedgwick has a useful definition of queerness as 'the open mesh of possibilities, gaps, overlaps, dissonances and resonances', where 'the constituent elements of anyone's gender, of anyone's sexuality, aren't made (or *can't* be made) to signify monolithically.' Emil was a possibility, so was Peggy, so were the other lovers Hart met with and made love with, however fleetingly.

They intended to return to Mexico, Peggy said, after two years in New York, including a period of rehabilitation for Hart. The following morning, full of apologies and promises, Hart presented Peggy with another corsage. It was 'large enough to satisfy a Hollywood queen'. They toured their favourite market one last time, Hart whispering stories in her ear. Daniel presented Peggy and Hart with flowers from the garden as they left. Hart promised that he would send for Daniel and his family once they reached New York.

The Overcoat

There are many stories clustered around Hart Crane's death. Some fragments:

The overcoat was folded over the railing;
It was discarded;
The overcoat was thrown over the railing, almost falling.
　The belt streamed through the bars;
I must correct you, it was a light topcoat, not a jacket;
The sea was glassy, calm. Beaufort 0: smoke rises
　vertically;
There were waves. Beaufort 4: small waves, becoming
　larger; fairly frequent white horses. Raises dust and
　loose paper, small branches are moved;
His cabin door was nailed shut that night. He escaped,
　went to pick up a sailor below decks and he was
　beaten;
He had been beaten, blackmailed, many times;

He said 'goodbye everyone!';
It was an accident, he fell drunk;
It was a threat – to get a reaction – like the iodine;
He waved from the water then disappeared;
He was silent, braced his legs against the railings and
    steeled himself for a moment;
He disappeared between the waves as the lifeboats
    searched for him;
It was a fit of melancholy;
It was the inevitable end to his suffering;
It was impulsive; regret must have flooded him;
His uncle was told first, wired a message by a passenger;
Blackadder looked out from the bridge with his
    binoculars;
Blackadder said a shark got him;
Blackadder said the blades ground him to mincemeat;
'Crane went overboard: body not found', stated the
    ship's radio report;
Grace paid to release Hart's belongings;
Grace had the overcoat dry-cleaned;
Marsden Hartley made an elegy out of paint: eyes in the
    sea, a shark with a red slash of a mouth.

There were headlines, syndicated in papers across the United States; some made their way to his mother at the Carleton Hotel in Chicago:

Student Poet Drowns At Sea
Poet Lost At Sea, Is Air Report
Crane, Hailed As Great Poet At 32, Drowned
Hart Crane, Poet, Vanishes From Ship New York Bound

Poet Leaped Into Sea, Ship Reports: Crane was
    Despondent Over Money and Poesy, Companion Says
Quits a Prosaic World: Tragedy of Hart Crane Revealed
    When Ship Docks
Hart Crane, Poet, Lost At Sea From Liner
Crane Chose His Death At Sea
Ohio Poet Lost On Sea Voyage
Poet Crane Lost At Sea, Message From Ship Says

Peggy's account of Hart's death was published in 1961. It has
the air of an adolescent play, wrapping up the complexities of
their relationship into neat parcels. Plot holes and doubts are
explained away with hammy efficiency. Peggy stages a number
of unnatural conversations with Hart in the piece:

> I'll wire for rooms in the morning. It will be a nice place
> for a brief honeymoon. Your divorce papers should be
> there by then, and we can get married immediately. I've
> given you a hard time with my wildness. Perhaps I can
> make it up to some extent. Cleveland I can take if you are
> with me. It won't be for long.

What is known is that it was hot in Veracruz. The breeze on
the *Orizaba* was a relief. Hart introduced Peggy to the officers
as they walked along the decks. She noticed their raised
eyebrows. It was a Sunday, 24 April. They would have the whole
day in Havana. They would reach the city the next morning.
Hart loved Havana. He had loved it as a boy, when he first
visited the Isle of Pines with his mother. And at twenty-six,
when he had visited the island as he tried to finish *The Bridge*.
Hart would curb his drinking for a few days. He would not

drink in Havana, he promised. Or, at least, he would wait until they sat down to eat. He knew a good restaurant where the waiters spoke English. Peggy could go shopping and he would meet her there. He looked strong, Peggy thought. He was making plans for New York: they would only stay a few days. Hotel Lafayette would do – in the Village so they could meet friends, if he felt up to it; word of his behaviour with Porter had got back to them. Hart would stop by his publisher, Boni & Liveright. Peggy would travel upstate to organise her house.

Hart was looking forward, she thought, and this time with a sense of reality. The speculative, dark vision he had of the future seemed to be lessening its hold on him. He had come to think the worst-case scenarios that he imagined were inevitable. These future visions seemed as real as the decking boards, or the blue wash of the sea, or the sting of alcohol at the back of the throat. In truth, our predictions of what might come to be are our own fictions. We may as well imagine the best-case scenario, instead of living the worst twice: once in our imaginations, and once in reality.

They slept well both nights before their arrival in Havana, sprawled in Peggy's cabin. On Tuesday morning, the Morro Castle drifted past the porthole. After breakfast, they headed ashore. The morning was fresh and 'brittle', Peggy recalled. Peggy went shopping, picking up a bundle of records for Hart as a surprise. She arrived at the restaurant. He was not there. It was cool, and she set down her bags to wait, nibbling on a sandwich. He did not arrive. The boat was due to leave soon. She ordered a cab.

Hart was waiting for her on the ship. He had waited for Peggy in a different restaurant, scribbling a postcard to Aunt Sally – his final written words:

Off here for a few hours on my way home. Will write you soon. Am going back to Cleveland to help in the business crisis.

There had been some kind of confusion. 'He has been on the ship for over an hour,' the purser told her, stood on the gang-plank eyeing the crowds. She was exhausted, and headed straight to her own room where she set down her shopping. Her arms ached. She washed and changed for dinner. He was probably drinking somewhere. The simplest explanation was probably the most likely. She would take the records and enjoy them for herself on the phonograph in the bar. She ordered a highball, watching the bartender mix whisky, soda and a little citrus syrup. She sipped her drink and selected a record, turning up the volume as loud as she could, barely registering the bartender's comment that Hart was looking for her once again. There was a pretty box of Cuban matches propped against a stack of coasters. Perching a cigarette between her lips, she struck the box with a match. It exploded, sending flames around her hands and wrist and up her arm. She fainted.

The bartender carried Peggy to the doctor's office. 'Burned badly,' she heard someone say. She could feel the doctor wrapping her arm in a bandage and an ointment – it smelled earthy, like tannic acid. Hart arrived. He was furious and drunk. She was careless, he said. She was magnificently clumsy, incredible for such a tiny person. The doctor chased Hart from his office and poured Peggy a large whisky.

Hart wouldn't let Peggy sleep. He kept reappearing at the door of the doctor's office. This time he blamed the ship, or the matches. He would sue. He would sue the match company. He would sue the ship's staff for negligence. Appearing once again, he tried to carry Peggy from the office to her room but she refused, clutching medicine from the doctor and holding the wall for support instead. In her cabin, she got into bed. Hart left.

Hart reappeared, peering round her door. It was hard to say how much time had passed. Perhaps five minutes. Perhaps an hour. He left. The doctor visited with more medication. Then Hart reappeared, sounding distraught. Blackadder arrived: 'Will you give me the authority to lock Mr Crane in his cabin?' 'Yes, yes,' she said. Why not before? 'Please just do it,' she begged the captain.

Somehow, he escaped. He made his way below deck. What happened next is unknown, but he emerged badly beaten. At 4 a.m. he was locked in his cabin for a final time. William Carlos Williams, writing over a decade later, claimed that Hart had been 'deceived and thrashed', implying that a pick-up had gone wrong.

Hart was persuaded into his room. The door was nailed shut. Peggy slept. She wrote her version of the following morning in her essay, the majority of the story taking place within the confines of her cabin. When she woke, she wondered if any of it had happened. It was Wednesday 27 April. Hart appeared in her doorway once again. He was sober, but seemed anxious. He couldn't remember anything. His wallet was missing – a ring was missing.

He needed a drink. Peggy agreed – he would get sick otherwise – but insisted he eat a large breakfast first. Hart tried to explain what had happened in Havana: she had gone to the wrong restaurant, he claimed, so he came back and started to drink on the ship. He ate quickly: cereal, bacon, toast, grapefruit. Peggy watched him. He hadn't had dinner the night before. She sent him off to get ready for the day. The steward-ess, in a heavily starched white shirt, brushed Peggy's hair care-fully, arranging the tawny strands around her face.

He returned, still in his pyjamas, and sat down on the bed. Over the thin fabric, he had on a light topcoat worn like a robe. Peggy suggested that he might shave and try once again to dress. He would feel better, surely, once he was in clean clothes. 'I'm not going to make it, dear, I'm utterly disgraced,' he said. Perhaps he was remembering. 'All right, dear. Good-bye,' he said. He closed the door. The stewardess helped Peggy into a dress that would accommodate her bandage. 'What would you like for lunch?' she asked.

There was a loud noise, a blast: the ship's whistle. The boat stopped, the machinery crunching as it slowed. She knew it was him. She ran upstairs with the stewardess, clutching her arm. Long ropes were moving: lifeboats were being lowered into the water. The doctor ran past. An officer ran up to her and spoke. His mouth was moving, but she couldn't hear him at first. 'The captain requests that you come to the bridge,' he said. It was noon.

Peggy was disparaged after Hart's death. As a heavy drinker herself, she was roundly blamed for an increase in Hart's alco-hol consumption. Both Grace and Sam blamed her for Hart's decline, and Grace blocked Peggy from any involvement in the editing of Hart's posthumous manuscripts. An early letter of Grace's to Sam, written in the exhaustion of grief, has a clear instruction pencilled at the top: 'Be sure to destroy this letter at <u>once</u>.' In it, she rages at Peggy, after finding explicit love letters written to Hart. Her son was 'innate refinement & delicacy personified'. She was appalled that he would receive letters of such 'rank profanity' – even worse than what she had 'read in French work'. Sam and Grace shared a sense that his relationship with Peggy had caused an 'injury to his psyche'. She was a 'very dangerous woman, sexually pathological, and alcoholic', Grace said, forming her view of Peggy after reading a useful, if guarded, letter from Anita Brenner.

'I think we may regard his death as an accident', wrote Hart's friend Bill Wright to Grace in June, 'not in the usual sense of course, but in the sense that we would regard typhoid fever, for instance, as an accident.' Hart's Uncle Madden told a reporter that: 'He expected to stay a few days in New York before coming here for a long rest.' He tried to comfort Grace, telling her that: 'We can only regret that Hart thought that there was anything which would warrant his taking the step he did.'

These more sensitive, humane comments did not become part of the story of Hart's death. Writing in the *New Republic* shortly after Hart's death, his friend and Peggy's estranged husband, Malcolm Cowley, wrote:

> . . . he sat in his closed cabin playing the phonograph, as he used to do when composing a poem; but this time he was meditating a poem of a different sort, a poem of action which the world could interpret in its own fashion . . . Did he carry some secret with him into the ocean – into that 'great wink of eternity,' that 'superscription of bent foam and wave' which he celebrated so often in his poems?

Cowley quotes phrases from the 'Voyages' in his obituary, trying to make his death mean something. He suggests that

Hart's death was 'a poem of action', a version of performance art, that he dived into his great muse, the ocean, to die. This troubling idea was reiterated in a profusion of elegies written for Hart following his death where poets had him 'jump', 'To trace the visionary company of love', after a 'vision' that 'he could never attain'. A newspaper article made the claim that he 'had taken seriously the philosophy of a famous contemporary, Edna St. Vincent Millay, when she wrote: "Mine is a body that should die at sea."' William Carlos Williams, a doctor as well as a poet, wrote that Hart had 'got to the end of his method', that 'he was returning to create and he created nothing'. Williams, who referred to Hart as a 'crude homo' in letters, claimed that the dead poet's method was nothing but 'excrescence', that is to say, an abnormal profusion.

Cowley, like the other friends who paid tribute to him in the pages of fashionable literary journals and newspapers, was also one of Hart's chief literary critics and interpreters of his poetry. The myth of Hart Crane sprang into action. His death was romanticised – 'the Shelley of my age', wrote Robert Lowell some twenty years later, a poet taught and mentored by Allen Tate. His poetry was read backwards, through the prism of his death. 'Voyages' became a collection of self-elegies, rather than love poems, that foreshadowed Hart's sea-death.

Grace declared these essays 'stupid pieces of morbidity' after reading a particularly egregious offering by Gorham Munson, a friend of Hart's in the early 1920s. They upset Sam, watching his friend, 'a realistic person', being converted 'into a legend', his complexity erased through focus on his dark moods. He cut off contact with Hart's first biographer, Philip Horton, on reading *Hart Crane: The Life of an American Poet*, published in 1937. 'Horton seems to have been oblivious to the fact that

Hart was not a morbid human being, except under the influence of drink', Sam explained to John Unterecker, who worked on *Voyager: A Life of Hart Crane* over the next decade. 'A' life shows the biographer acknowledging they have written a version of Hart; 'The' is an attempt to be definitive, a subtle denial of the biographer's own deeply subjective position. There are more biographers of Hart: Clive Fisher's in *Hart Crane: A Life* and Paul Mariani's in *The Broken Tower: The Life of Hart Crane*.

We cannot know why Hart stepped off the *Orizaba* as he returned home. 'There are strange conditions in our lives', C.A. had told him. Strange conditions are a constant. What can change is our ability to withstand them. Hart had clearly experienced turbulent moods throughout his life, and had been living through a period of complex distress, with the death of his father, alienation from his mother, progressive alcoholism, lack of progress on his new epic, a turbulent relationship, returning to the United States during the Depression – his friends severely beaten up as they attempted to get food to striking miners in Kentucky. But his last year was not a simple precipitous decline. Rather, the weeks ebbed and flowed with sadness and various joys: his garden, hiking, discovering Mexican artistic culture, festivals, a significant new poem, lovers, armfuls of flowers, flea markets, new friends, pottery, jewellery.

Joseph Brodsky wrote that:

It's an abominable fallacy that suffering makes for greater art. Suffering blinds, deafens, ruins, and often kills. Osip Mandelstam was a great poet before the revolution. So was Anna Akhmatova, so was Marina Tsvetaeva. They would have become what they became even if none of the historical events that befell Russia in this century had taken place: because they were *gifted*. Basically, talent doesn't need history.

What Brodsky means is that talent will find an out. Mandelstam, Akhmatova, and Tsvetaeva might have been catalysed by their environments, but they would always, Brodsky suggests, have become writers, no matter their experiences. But what they write about depends on their environment. By extension of his argument, so many potential writers and artists are lost to suffering, their talent wasted. I wince a little at the idea of 'talent', rather than hard work, reading and revision.

Whether or not we need 'history' to write, we are all enmeshed within our own historical moments. Of course, Hart's experiences were markedly different than Akhmatova's, the most gorgeous poet:

> Do you forgive me these November days?
> In canals around the Neva fires fragment.
> Scant is tragic autumn's finery.

But Hart lived through a period of sexual censoriousness that pressed upon him from every angle, family and friends. He was beaten and blackmailed and estranged from his mother. I write as a heterosexual woman within a markedly changed society. Certain laws have changed, but the homophobes, transphobes and prigs are on the march. They strategise, carving out positions within our culture and conversations that allow them to affect intellectual persecution.

Hart's poetry is inextricable from the censoriousness of his times, but also finds its own resistant energy in its fugitive attempts to explore his romantic and erotic experiences. The central feature of his poetry, the logic of metaphor, emerged through his attempts to write about his lovers in allusive and associative ways, avoiding censorship and condemnation. His metaphors conceal and reveal through a range of complex and easily decoded images: 'exclaim receive / The secret oar and petals of all love.'

Psychological suffering is a wasting disease. It is exhausting; time runs fast and slow. It is, ultimately, an adversary not a muse. In 'O Carib Isle' Hart writes of his ongoing struggle to write from within such agony:

> The wind that knots itself in one great death –
> Coils and withdraws. So syllables want breath.

Psychological pain is figured as a wind, coiling and abstracted, but its presence is felt through its actions on other objects (the wind whipping up grains of white sand on the beach), which is to say that anxiety is a thought process rather than an entity. It will latch on to anything and work on it, reshaping thoughts until they are ugly and defamiliarised. It withdraws and Hart reminds himself that writing ('syllables') requires 'breath' (life). Death might mean the absence of this gale-like distress, but it means the poet falling quiet. Death was not the poem as action. It was just silence.

Ennoia and Ophis

Grace poured sand onto the Victrola. Grains lodged in the grooves of the spinning disc, some slipping onto the wooden table. Through the morning, a scattered, yellowish ring had formed on the carpet, interrupted at the spot where she stood. She watched the record tilt to the left under its uneven weight. The oboe's delicate movements – a sound that ordinarily would propel the music forward – stretched into an embarrassing plaintive drone and the drumbeats became slow, deep scratches. She turned the hand crank a few times and waited, humming faintly as the sand shifted a little. Nothing.

It was cold out, but the sun through the window was still generous and warm on her eyelids and the high points of her cheeks. For a moment, the yellow sun seemed to have the same quality as the light that streamed through the window in Garrettsville, where Hart was born. The arbour would shake slightly in the wind as she held him on the porch, sheening her forehead with droplets. It was a soft yellow: diving, her son would say, it dives through the wet leaves, the wet grass. He saw the sun in apples, she thought, and in the shape of her eyelids.

Hart wrote this way, chanting fragments until they formed verses. He let the increasing speed of Maurice Ravel's 'Boléro' (a favourite) pull him into anxious repetitions.

> I saw the frontiers gleaming of his mind;
> or are there frontiers – running sands sometimes
> running sands – somewhere – sands running . . .

He piled sand onto the record until the music slouched to a halt, 'interminably / long since somebody's nickel – stopped playing – '

Nothing. Hart was garrulous with the clairvoyant, but would not come to her alone. Frances was full of talk of his new poem, fathers, complex spiritual theories, Hart's lovers, the alignments of the stars, a peacock called Mr Jackson, and even her diet, urging her to resist meat, cheese, milk, cane sugar and fermented liquids. Frances said Hart left bunches of flowers by their beds. Jasmine by Frances's pillow and gardenias at his own, wherever he was. Violets for her – her favourite.

Hart returned to violets in his poems. But they tended to be associated with death, or decay. Yes, there was a 'syphilitic selling violets calmly' in the subway station. And in 'Pastorale', which begins 'No more violets, / And the year / Broken into smoky panels.' He wrote:

> If dusty, I bear
> An image beyond this
> Already fallen harvest,

I can only query, 'Fool –
Have you remembered too long;

Or was there too little said
For ease or resolution –
Summer scarcely begun
And violets,
A few picked, the rest dead?'

He was so young when he wrote these lines, just twenty-two. At first they seemed to be about his struggle with his own poetic voice – the risk in bearing an image, stretching comparisons and associations to their limits. But the violets, and the violets at her pillow, reminded Grace of C.A. Yes, there was too little said between them – or too much, at times. C.A. had given her flowers on wilted, thin stems. Another attempt to reunite – failed, of course. They both remarried. She divorced, again. C.A. died. Two Mrs Cranes, the younger a widow. Her son mourned by a mother and a stepmother practically Hart's age, a woman she had never met. She poured herself a large glass of gin. It was her third. She would need to be up early tomorrow, but it didn't matter any more.

Hart had fed them a poem, meeting by meeting. They had received it as automatic scribbles, which she worked with, typing it up. Occasionally Frances would receive a full verse, her eyelashes fluttering and pupils shifting quickly behind. She had it somewhere here. The front page was a little greasy, with her prints smudged all over it. The title: 'Ennoia and Ophis'. Frances had tried to explain its significance, but, like many of her son's poems, it sent Grace to the library. The title page: 'Dedicated to All Mothers and in particular my beloved Mother

Grace Hart Crane Without whose vision and sacrifice this testament could not have been Incarnated.'

The Ophites were Christian Gnostics, she discovered. The Gnostics emerged in Jewish and early Christian sects in the first century. Gnosticism was an esoteric heresy that sought salvation not through faith but through the acquisition of mysterious knowledge. These forms of knowledge ranged from complex theories of the universe to the mind. The Ophites had their own sprawling Gnostic theology, worshipping the serpent. The snake (Ophis in biblical Greek) represented a higher god, offering knowledge (Ennoia) and, with it, liberation. The Ophites were first described in the *Syntagma*, a lost work by Hippolytus of Rome, who lived and wrote in the late second and early third centuries. The traces of the lost work are borne through accounts of the Ophites using Hippolytus as their source in works by Pseudo-Tertullian, Philastrius, Epiphanius, Origen, Clement of Alexandria, and Irenaeus, a Greek bishop who gathered together these stories in *Against Heresies*, recording them to refute their theological arguments.

Grace was packing again. It was 1944, three years after records of the seances end. The final meeting had been grossly hot; New York in July. They had received a series of instructions for a book that would include both the poems and theological lessons they had received over the last year. The title was 'REVELATIONS by HART CRANE', to be written vertically down the front cover. The first portion of the book would deal with her experiences of the seances, 'in the most impersonal manner possible'. Then the poems and lessons would follow.

She bound up the papers and slipped them into a file. Here were the books, which she slotted one by one into a case. One, tawny brown and black, was Emily Dickinson. It was a gift from Hart. *February 1927*, she had written inside. He loved Dickinson. She flicked through the volume, pausing at the sections she had annotated over almost two decades. A long, vibrating line hung around one poem:

> Heaven is what I cannot reach!
> The apple on the tree,
> Provided it do hopeless hang,
> That 'heaven' is, to me.
>
> The color on the cruising cloud,
> The interdicted ground
> Behind the hill, the house behind, –
> There Paradise is found!

Her son: 'The apple on its bough is her desire'. Her poems could be glimpsed through his, even Dickinson's breath, caught or relieved with these dashes. Hart learned from this, preserving his own in the 'Voyages', leaving traces of his living, breathing body behind on the page. There were more squiggles and lines. Notes that, I would imagine, she made after Hart left her cottage in California in 1928: 'If I could see you in a year, / I'd wind the months in balls.' And perhaps annotations made after he died: 'This world is not conclusion; / A sequel stands beyond' – the ligature was spiky, urgent. She clapped the book shut.

It was Leonia, New Jersey, this time. She had been engaged to help an elderly woman run her house, cleaning, cooking and running errands. No doubt she would need to care for her too. She had not told Sam she was leaving. It was too humiliating. It would not be her last job. She grew weary of the woman. By April 1946 she was in Manhasset, Long Island, where she cooked and cleaned from 6 a.m. for a woman 'obsessed' with dirt. At some point, she returned to the city for a brief spell. Brom Weber, Hart's second biographer, tracked her down at the Sutton Hotel at 330 East 56th Street. She refused help, preferring to keep working. During her last year she accepted one last job. In the spring of 1947 she returned to New Jersey. For $15 a month she took charge of a household in New Milford with two children who she found spoiled. At some point during these final years, she started drinking heavily. By July she had been hospitalised.

The poem Frances delivered in their dark-lit meetings reads like a misguided pastiche of Hart's writing by someone who had misunderstood it. It slips into awkward archaisms (the first line: 'With those whose blood from common source doth run') as the poem attempts to inhabit the voice of *The Bridge* ('Thee, across the harbor, silver paced', 'Thou hand of fire') and clumsily manipulating the grammar of the lines to reach a rhyme:

> Be gone Joy! Thou are a two faced wretch –
> A smiling Messalina – whose sole delight
> Is gaping men – who by imagination's stretch
> Have called thee mistress, in thy lures bedight.

There is little value in the text as a poem, which requires wading through vague Spiritualistic images of abjection ('a worm that crawls the ground') and joy ('Joy borne of the gods in their descent / From high Olympic grandeur'). It is a bad poem, patchworking fragments of quotation from Hart's poems with esoteric theological assertions that map onto Gnostic cosmology. 'Blood' from a 'common source', for instance, echoes Hart's erotic images of 'mingling blood' in 'Voyages', while the line 'Pain cuts the rose and round its stem is ravelled' recalls images of roses and wreathes in 'Cutty Sark', and 'imagination's stretch' echoes Hart's 'The imagination spans beyond despair'. The poem ends as the serpent, Ophis, speaks 'the Master Word – Ennoia', communicating absolute knowledge, figured as a ray of light passing through a prism.

Because the seances were recorded in notes taken by each attendant and involved a variety of methods of communication – table tipping, automatic writing, singing, spoken messages – determining the authorship of the poem is impossible. It is blended, a mixture of hands went into it. The seance records show that the verses emerged first through Frances. 'Take the verses as I give them to you', Frances declared as Hart. 'I will try to reach you alone but if not possible to do so, you must have patience and persevere each time you come. We need Frances – for your work. She is an easy channel.'

The message bearers did not just include Hart, but ranged from Shelley, Sappho, the Spiritualist theologian Oliver Lodge, Theona, the wife of Pythagorus and Paul the Apostle, with Byron in the background in one meeting. Even if we were to believe that these voices were truly present in these seances, there are many layers of intervention between the voice and the final typed document. A message had to pass through Frances, with notes taken by Grace, sometimes with ideas pulled out of the scribbles of automatic writing. Grace would then type up any notes, or would sit for hours deciphering automatic writing: wobbly lines with words or shapes taking up a whole page. Looking at the originals, I could not see letters no matter how I arranged the page. Each could be seen to resemble any letter or word, with enough of a squint.

In this way, Grace is the final author if not the sole author of the poem. These pages form a document of her own grief, both in their record of her process of seeking out a medium, and the preservation of the heart-breaking conversations between mother and this composite version of her son, which seems to have been formed through Frances's reading of Hart's poems, and her conversations with Grace. Reading 'Ennoia and Ophis' in Grace's voice rather than that of her son makes the lines reform: 'pain wrecks her', she writes, 'intent on death my soul impaling'. 'Thou alone canst make this awful night repent', thinking of Hart's final hours, perhaps. Her own creative frustrations emerge in the final lines of the poem:

> Crash and crush against the barrier –
> Beat and bruise the battered spirit –

Grace seemed to believe that the poem was written by her son, or perhaps she could not quite take ownership of her own work. She tried to have 'Ennoia and Ophis' included in a new edition of Hart's *Collected Poems*, writing to Waldo Frank. Frank, whose letters to Hart were invariably warm and generous, was similarly kind and sincere in his responses to Grace. But he urged her to keep the documents sealed. The seances were common knowledge among Hart's friends; Sam had attended some meetings, and Grace entrusted the seance document to him after her death. Bill Wright considered writing about these seances, but worried that any attention to them might damage Hart's reputation. Besides, they might have been 'merely a figment of her increasing illness and infirmity', he wrote to Sam, 'it would hardly do to put any stress on them'.

Grace held on to Hart's friends too tightly. She was angry when Waldo Frank and Sam took their time to respond. At first Frank tried to console her, apologising for hurting her feelings, then he worked to detach himself from the friendship. Sam was more patient, withstanding her threats and manipulations. Grace had a peculiar sense of loyalty that was impossible for those around her to fulfil. 'Don't live to regret your attitude towards me', she would write to Sam, as she had her son. She saw herself almost as Sam's mother, and so she reverted to her old methods, her old ways of showing and securing affection. Sam was patient in response, as he had been with Hart when he, too, had tested the limits of their friendship.

Grace and Sam became close after Hart's death. They had known each other since Hart was a boy and Sam still worked at Laukhuff's, but they bonded in their grief. Many of Hart's friends wrote to Grace after his death (Frank, Tate, Brenner, Crosby, Bill Wright, the various Bobs), but she bonded tightly with Sam. 'I would not talk to anyone but you, like this,' Grace told Sam. Through Sam, she tried to challenge Hart's claim that he had broken off their relationship after he disclosed his sexuality to her – a story known to his friends. They shared news; Grace wrote conveying her delight at seeing FDR at the Democratic National Convention, 'Many people feel that they cannot go on under the same conditions, and are willing to risk a change,' she told him. She disclosed to Sam the strange feelings that were coming to her as she waded through the bureaucracy of Hart's death. It cost a great deal for her to get Hart's belongings released. She unwrapped them carefully. 'He loved color', she explained, 'and certain little trifles had such a fascination for him.' Her letters to Sam show that Grace seems to have genuinely believed that Hart was present with her, in some other form. 'I feel this experience called death has awakened him to a clearer sense of life & its purpose and that somewhere he is happier and making progress,' she explained.

'If I must live without him', Grace wrote of her son, 'I must do it as bravely as possible.' In the autumn of 1933, she moved to New York to an apartment on Broadway. She met with Sam at least once a week. She fussed over Sam and his boyfriend, Pat, telling Sam's mother how wonderful it must be to see her son so happy, and how much she enjoyed spending time at their apartment, being tended to and having meals cooked for her. She worried Sam didn't eat enough, avoiding food when he felt anxious (which was all the time). Despite her foibles, Sam respected Grace. She had baby-watched and scrubbed floors to 'keep herself alive', he told Unterecker.

Sam died on 14 May 1976 in the New York Jewish Home and Hospital. His funeral was held in Cleveland. Sam's health had declined after a stroke that February. He protested about his move to the Jewish Home, insisting on returning to his apartment. Before he became so frail, he had conducted numerous interviews, trying to ensure that his memories of Grace and Hart were preserved. He was particularly troubled by Horton's account of Grace, and took pains to offer a testimony that might challenge this view. Sam's testimony has typically been treated as unreliable, in large part because he made errors cataloguing early poems by Hart, misattributing a weak sonnet to his friend.

I think of the character William Beckwith working with Lord Charles Nantwich's diaries in Alan Hollinghurst's *The Swimming Pool Library*, published on the cusp of Section 28. At first, Will is frustrated, 'irritated, almost piqued by the way the life in them went parochially on.' He expected the diaries to 'fall open at the dirty bits', for there to '*be* dirty bits'. Will finds himself living between the gaps that he sees in the diary, filling them in, almost, from his post-1967 existence, living in London fifteen years after the decriminalisation of homosexuality. Sam's stories may well be true. But perhaps it doesn't matter if Sam, talking in the 1970s, filled the gaps in Hart's life as he recounted stories as an elderly man. There is something to be gained from not quite knowing.

One afternoon in his last spring, a friend took Sam to the Gotham Book Mart. He couldn't climb the three steps out of the bookstore and up into the street. Faced with how weak he had become, he started to withdraw. Sam wrote his last poem in April, 'John Clare in 1864'. He imagined Clare in the last year of his life. 'Across the tethered portico, / The shadows come, the shadows go', wrote Sam. 'I'll follow in his flight.' He slipped into a coma on 8 May, aged eighty-nine.

As Grace lay dying in the summer of 1947, Sam visited her. She had cirrhosis of the liver and had fallen into a coma. She was in the Holy Name, a Catholic hospital in Teaneck, New Jersey. According to Sam, the Holy Name was the only hospital that would accept her.

In 1946, Grace had vanished. 'I had been on very intimate terms with her. She just disappeared,' Sam explained later. She had been scrubbing floors, raising children. They reconnected after Brom Weber tracked her down. Sam held on to Grace until the end. He has a suspiciously neat description of Grace's last moments. His story has made its way into portraits of Grace. Whether or not the scene he described happened, it suggests a great deal about how he, close to mother and son, understood their relationship.

Sam's account is as follows: he approached her side and she woke from her coma. They drank coffee together, or at least Grace tried. 'Who is this lady?' a nurse asked. 'She is the mother of a brilliant and wonderful American poet,' he told her. Grace started. 'What did you say about me?' she asked, irritated to find herself talked over, prone in her bed. Sam repeated the dialogue. 'Poor boy,' Grace said.

Hart's biographers have dwelled on that saccharine final phrase – supposedly her last words. They see it as a moment of salvation, an apology of sorts. But Sam included Grace's anger. 'What did you say about me?' she says. She was provoked by Sam's description, seeing herself refracted once again through her son in her final moments. As Virginia Woolf writes of the women on the periphery of great men: 'one often catches a glimpse of them in the lives of the great, whisking away into the background, concealing, I sometimes think, a wink, a laugh, perhaps a tear.' Grace's irritation reveals her doubled loss: that of her son, and of her own fulfilment. The mother of a wonderful American poet; a woman concealed in the background of a great man.

Grace's life has been broken down into components by Hart's biographers. A girl, a fiancée, a wife, a mother, divorced, a wife again, a mother without her son, her own death. This makes sense narratively, from the point of view of the poet's biographer. I find it terrifying, a narrative trap. It is easy to do this, to partition our lives into eras. All too invested in narrative structures, I have absorbed these designs, thinking of myself as different pre and past traumatic event, pre and past lovers. The narrative blocks begin with a first moment, they end with another, contained by these parameters. I am not a mother. I wonder if this would bring another set of constraints, partitions of the mind. Or if I could transcend them. Grace couldn't. Many women I have known couldn't, can't.

The summer before I arrived at UCL, as I was slipping down into the unnamed darkness, I became obsessed with Graham Greene. I was working as a secretary in the bus department of the local council, spending my days proofreading timetables and pamphlets. After work I walked to the Oxfam bookshop, working my way through the Greene shelf. I read *The Power and the Glory*, I read *The End of the Affair*, I read everything I could, sitting with a large, sweet coffee on my lunch break in the nearby cathedral grounds.

The End of the Affair opens: 'A story has no beginning or end: arbitrarily one chooses that moment of experience from which to look back or from which to look ahead.' I wish I had read him more carefully. What we understand as our beginnings and endings are a choice. I can choose the peak of the narrative myself. I can choose any number of beginnings or endings, and look forwards and backwards at Hart, Grace, and myself from different angles. The shape of it will change as I change, feeling better, worse, different, more or less in touch with what is and what is not real. Perhaps that 'remorseless line' between myself in a rational and irrational state is best understood as amorphous and vast, the white-tipped edge of a wave that comes into the harbour and drags itself back out to sea, grasping at the stones. I toe the shoreline. Perhaps recovery looks like watchfulness.

Grace died on 30 August 1947, the day after Sam's visit. Sam became the executor of the estates of both Hart and Grace, in possession of their manuscripts and letters. She left $40 behind. Sam gave her clothes to the poor. Grace was cremated. Sam walked across the Brooklyn Bridge with Brom Weber and Arthur Pell, who worked for Hart's publisher. Sam scattered her ashes, the dust rising with 'inviolate curve, forsake our eyes'. Apparitional she rose into the air, building and lifted high over the chained water of the East River. This way, Sam imagined, she might join her son. For a moment, the dust altered the music made by the wind on the wires.

Acknowledgements

This book was written with financial support from the Arts Council of Ireland, for which I am truly grateful. My thanks to the wonderful staff at the Tyrone Guthrie Centre, where I finished the manuscript.

Thanks to all at Artellus, particularly my agent, Leslie Gardner, for helping me assemble my ideas for this book, for finding it a home, and for her enthusiasm and support throughout.

My thanks to Kate Craigie and Abi Scruby, my editors, and to everyone at John Murray Originals. I am so grateful to Abi for her skill in shaping the book and helping me find its final form. Thanks to Martin Bryant for his brilliant copy-editing, and to Laurence Cole for his proofreading.

My thanks to my early readers, Megan Girdwood, Suzannah V. Evans, and Camilla Sutherland. Thanks to Tim Curtis and Philippa Morris at the Little Apple Bookshop for giving me a job and for their encouragement during the earliest stages of this project.

Thanks very much to Cormac O'Malley for facilitating

research on his father. A huge thanks to the archivists and librarians who have helped me with this project. I am particularly grateful to the librarians at Columbia Rare Book and Manuscript Library for their kindness and patience. My thanks to my teachers over the years.

All love to my friends. My love to my family: my parents, Felicity and Alan James, my brother Christopher, my Grandma, Dorcas Gould, and my almost-sister, Katherine Riedel. My biggest and final thanks to Karl O'Hanlon, for his tireless encouragement and belief and for thinking with me, always. I would not have written this book without him.

Notes and Sources

I provide the notes below in cases where sources are not self-evident. Hart's and Grace's movements have been pieced together through letters, the reminiscences of friends, newspapers and magazine articles, and existing biographies and narratives of the period. I am indebted to Hart Crane's biographers, Philip Horton, Brom Weber, John Unterecker, Paul Mariani and Clive Fisher. I used Marc Simon's edition of Hart Crane's poems throughout. Unless indicated otherwise, quotations from letters are taken from the editions listed in the bibliography. I have silently corrected the erratic spelling in Hart's letters. Correspondence between Grace and Hart's friends is held in her files in the Hart Crane archive (Columbia). Readers seeking further details are very welcome to contact me through John Murray.

Introduction: The Remorseless Line

The phrase 'remorseless line' appears in 'The Wine Menagerie'; 'searching, thumbing', 'The Tunnel'; 'In all the argosy', 'Voyages

V'; 'Permit me voyage, love', 'Voyages III'. See Malcolm Cowley, *A Second Flowering*, on Hart's associative thought patterns and the Patterson weekend. Fisher notes Hart's visit to the *New Republic*. Hart's Guggenheim application is in his papers at Columbia. Grace and Loveman discuss Hart's collecting habits in letters (Crane Papers and Sam Loveman papers, Columbia); Madden's telegram is among Grace's files. Rosanna Warren, Warner Berthoff, and Paul Mariani wrote letters to the *New York Times* in response to Logan's article. On 'intimate details', Esmé Weijun Wang's *The Collected Schizophrenias* suggested how I might carve out boundaries when writing about mental illness and trauma. Lesley Simpson, 'Mexico killed Hart', as quoted in Unterecker. The idea of 'excavation' is informed by Sylvia Plath's 1963 BBC interview ('one should be able to control and manipulate experiences'). On 'the logic of metaphor' see 'A Discussion with Hart Crane', 'General Aims and Theories'; 'choiring strings' is from 'To Brooklyn Bridge'. For intimacy see Berlant; for the queer archive, Mircir; for versions of poets, McLane; on rhyme see Hill on 'the gravitational pull of words' in 'A Pharisee to Pharisees'. 'Negative capability' appears in Keats's letters.

Chapter 1: Party on the *Orizaba*

Zinsser recalls his friendship with Hart in *Rats, Lice and History* and *As I Remember Him*. 'The doctor has thrown . . . harbor' fragment is found in *As I Remember Him*. Hart's letters refer to symptoms of alcohol withdrawal and delirium tremens. For American visions of 1930s Havana see Walker Evans's photographs. On 'brown eyes': Hart's appearance is described on his US army registration card (submitted two months before Armistice, he did not serve). Shelley's lines are from 'Music when Soft Voices Die (To--)'.

Chapter 2: 'Why do you not come to me alone?'

The chapter title is a quotation from Grace's seance transcript, which exists in two versions: 1) Hart Crane Papers at Columbia University (typed) and 2) Grace Crane Collection of Automatic Writing Attributed to Hart Crane (handwritten). I quote from the former throughout. On Hart Crane and queer modernism see Thomas Yingling and Niall Munro. Grace describes destroying Hart's letters in correspondence with Loveman. See also Fisher on letters that 'had any bearing on her son's sexual temper'. For Nathan Asch see Unterecker. I base the description of the attack on Hart and Emil on Hart's letter to Susan and William Slater Brown, 27 March 1928. Elizabeth Hart is described by Loveman in *Hart Crane: A Conversation*. Towne House menu in Grace's files (Columbia). Grace and Charles Curtis's divorce and Grace's finances in Unterecker. Quotation from Eileen Myles, 'hart!'

Chapter 3: Debts

Hart mentions visiting Rivera's murals in a letter to Cowley. *Sleeping Gull* appears in a 1926 letter from Hart to Lachaise. For Hart's 1930 earnings see Unterecker. Finances contextualised using Cowley's *Exile's Return*. The 'Precari' jotter is Hart's *Vocabulary Notebook* in the Columbia archive. *El Universal* interview translated by Camilla Sutherland.

Chapter 4: Friends

For Paz's childhood see his Nobel Prize speech and *Itinerary*. For the Virgin of Guadalupe and Juan Diego see Matovina, *Theories of Guadalupe*, and Porter, *Uncollected Early Prose*. For Paz 'La Torre Rota' see *Versiones y diversiones*. For Porter's biography see *Conversations with Katherine Anne Porter* (Lopez) and Walsh. Quotations from Porter's letters are from Walsh throughout, unless otherwise specified. Hart describes the bridle vaguely as 'ancient'. Peggy is more specific, explaining in *Robber Rocks* that 'it had been worn by one of the conquistadors, of course.' The sketch of Hart in Greenwich Village is based on his disguised appearance in Brooks, *Hints to Pilgrims* (1921). On Best-Maugard's artistic practice see his *A Method for Creative Design*. 'Spiritual renewal' is Siqueiros's translated phrase from his 1921 manifesto in *Vida Américana*. For Rivera and Kahlo see Alcántara and Egnolff. For Sáenz's biography see Hamann, *Moisés Sáenz: vigencia de su Legado*. For Spratling's artistic practice see Morrill. Porter's 'He said once ... brutal shocks', 'I am Baudelaire', ' "Oh, don't!" ' are quotations from Lopez, *Conversations*; 'the romantic irresponsibility of drunkenness' is from a letter to Hart, 22 June 1931 (Maryland).

Chapter 5: The Towne House

For Hart's birthday card error see Horton and Fisher.

Chapter 6: Hart Crane's Flea Circus

For the American Field Service Ambulance Corps see Malcolm Cowley, *Exile's Return*. For Harry and Caresse Crosby see Hamalian. For Milton's linguistic inventions and patterns see Thomas Corns. Susan Jenkins Brown, as quoted in *Robber Rocks*. See Tate 'The Poet as Hero', 'A Poet, and his Life'. For sexuality and 'decadence' see Moore's interview with Hall. For Porter on Hart's 'vices' see Unrue, *Katherine Anne Porter Remembered* and Lopez, *Conversations*; 'brutality with brutality' as quoted in Walsh.

Chapter 7: The IRA Officer

For a biography of Ernie O'Malley, see Harry F. Martin and Cormac O'Malley. Quotations from O'Malley's letters from *Broken Landscapes* and archival correspondence with Hart and Harriet Monroe (Tamiment). See Eve Morrison on O'Malley and folklore in her essay in O'Malley's *The Men Will Talk to Me*; see Nicholas Allen on O'Malley's style in his introduction to *Broken Landscapes*. Hart's Helen appears in 'For the Marriage of Faustus and Helen'; Whitman, Emily Dickinson and Isadora Duncan are glimpsed in *The Bridge*. On Taos, see Dodge. O'Malley's syllabi are preserved in his archive; 'mountain . . . angles' is from 'Zuni Rocks'. 'Lack of language . . . spelt', O'Malley as quoted in English. Deportation statistics from US Citizen and Immigration Services Records. Boland's phrase is found in 'How We Made a New Art on Old Ground'. Archaeological details uncovered using the Government of Ireland Historic Environment Viewer. Hart's line 'shift, subvert' is from 'O Carib Isle'. For Greene, Walston and O'Malley see

Patten. Lines from a Swedish folk song, 'Längtan till Landet', by Herman Sätherberg, identified by my friend Ellinor Mattson.

Chapter 8: A Wedding

See Fisher on the Hart and Crane family histories and Unterecker for Hart's early years. Unterecker mentions C.A.'s amateur dramatics. Grace's year of birth is confirmed by the *Chicago Tribune* Marriage Licence announcement. Hart's maternal grandmother's name is confirmed using the *Beardsley Genealogy*. Grace's nightgown is held in the Hart Crane and Family Papers (Kent State). Fisher describes Hart's experiments with Grace's hats and Aunt Bess's reaction.

Chapter 9: Mixcoac Flower Garden

For Hart's early years see Unterecker. See Susan Jenkins Brown's *Robber Rocks* on Hart in Patterson. The phrase 'one floating flower' is from 'Voyages II'; 'ritual of sap and leaves', 'Pastorale'; the 'crash of leaves', *The Bridge*. Curators at Princeton University's Graphic Arts Department have identified the subject of Hart's poem to Sommer (an untitled still life in Princeton's collections). Loveman mentions Agrippenis in his interview with Unterecker (Unterecker Papers). Wright's last memory of Hart is described in a letter to Grace. Frank's comments appear in *In Search of Hart Crane*.

Chapter 10: Life Saver Candies

The 'cat sweeping through the waves' refers to Antonia Barber's *The Mousehole Cat*. 'The obvious questions', 'fund of knowledge' from Cormac O'Malley, 'Personal Note Searching for Ernie', *Broken Landscapes*. Colm Tóibín's chapter on Hart and Grace in *New Ways to Kill Your Mother*. Quotation from Freud's 1910 essay 'Leonardo Da Vinci', *Complete Works*, Vol XI. Adam Phillips on biography in his review essay, 'Roaring Boy'. Grunberg's comments on Hart and Grace in his Unterecker interview. C.A.'s death recorded in the *Akron Beacon Journal*. Sáenz's letter to Hart is located in Crane's Columbia archive. William Slater Brown recalls Hart's last trip to New York in *In Search of Hart Crane*.

Chapter 11: Isla de la Juventud

On the history of La Isla de la Juventud (the Isle of Pines) see Neagle. 'In plain view . . . bungalow', Harriet Taylor Upton, *A Twentieth Century History of Trumbull County, Ohio* as quoted in Fisher. Details of C.A.'s businesses and description of Aunt Sally in Fisher. 'Sun heap . . . underdrawers for owls', 'The Mango Tree'. 'Visibility is a trap', Foucault, *Discipline and Punish*. 'Adonis striding', Aunt Sally as quoted in Unterecker.

Chapter 12: Tepoztlán

Rivera's drawing of Tepotzlán is an illustration for Stuart Chase's *Mexico* (1931). On the legends and archaeology of Tepozteco and Tepoztlán, see Margarita Vargas-Betancourt. Lesley Simpson described Rourke as 'a queer, a fuzzy Marxist, and a sponger', as quoted in Fisher. For a history of the monastery see Tavarez. The description of the Aztec drum appears in Hart's letters.

Chapter 13: Siqueiros Comes to Stay

For Siqueiros's biography see Stein. Siqueiros ('My dinner . . . receive') and Blanca Luz Brum ('Not until . . . rips me') as quoted in Stein. Jolas translated by Camilla Sutherland. See Scott and Robinson on Taxco. 'Omissions are not accidents' was Moore's epigraph to her *Complete Poems*. Lesley Simpson as quoted in Unterecker.

Chapter 14: A Seance in New York

Grace's transcriptions are quotations from the seance document.

Chapter 15: Lovers

Love is 'piracy' is from 'Voyages V'; 'flung from dawn to dawn', 'Voyages III'; 'mutual blood', 'Voyages IV'; 'bright hair', 'eyes already sealed', and 'the slant of drifting foam', 'Voyages V'; 'And why do I often meet . . . on and on', 'The Tunnel'; 'Spry cordage', 'Voyages I'; 'There is some way . . . count the nights', 'For the Marriage of Faustus and Helen'; 'Permit me voyage', 'Voyages III'; 'Wounded by apprehensions', 'Possessions'. On desire as self-projection, see Lacan in *Desire and its Interpretation*. Grunberg's comment 'He was not a homosexual' appears in his Unterecker interview. Porter's letter is held in her archive. Her comments on Hart's 'twin vices' appear in *Katherine Porter Remembered*. 'Vapid': Moore to James Sibley Watson in her *Selected Letters*; 'discipline', Moore's interview with Hall. Brenner's 'Give to Caesar' is held in Crane's Columbia archive. For Peggy's biography, see Malcolm Cowley's *Exile's*

Return and Elizabeth Freer's biographical sketch available via the Alexander Street database. Quotations from Susan Jenkins Brown and Peggy Cowley, in Susan Jenkins Brown's *Robber Rocks*, but Peggy's 'great great person' comment is a scribbled note to Unterecker (Unterecker Papers). 'Eagle's nest' is Peggy's term. Loveman describes Opffer in his Unterecker interview. Quotations from Opffer's interview in the *Hart Crane Newsletter* (1.2). The line 'in the slant . . . long way home', 'Voyages V'; 'holy palmers kiss', *Romeo and Juliet*; 'your hands within . . . my tongue . . .', *The Bridge*. Loveman mentions arguments with Hart in his Unterecker interview. Lesley Simpson, Waldo Frank, Marian Simpson as quoted in Unterecker. Marian Simpson as quoted in Fisher, including comments on women and 'nuisances'. I include Peggy Cowley's dialogue as she remembers it in *Robber Rocks*.

Chapter 16: The Overcoat

The articles alluded to here are clippings in Hart Crane's archive (Columbia). Hartley's painting: *Eight Bells Folly: Memorial to Hart Crane* (1933). Susan Jenkins Brown's *Robber Rocks* contains Peggy Cowley's account (including dialogue). In her interview, Peggy told Unterecker that the purser had nailed Hart's cabin door shut the night before he died. Williams as quoted in Mariani. Grace's letters to Loveman detail Peggy Cowley's exclusion from involvement in his estate. Malcolm Cowley comments on 'the poem of action' in an unsigned article 'The Death of a Poet'; 'jump . . . never attain', Symons; Millay's poem is 'Burial'; Williams as quoted in Mariani, 'crude homo' in a letter to Ezra Pound (Pound papers); 'The Shelley of my age', Lowell's 'Words for Hart Crane'; Munson's article, 'A

Poet's Suicide and Some Reflections'. Akhmatova's poem takes
the first line as its title, 'Do you forgive me these November
days'. The lines 'exclaim receive . . . all love', 'Voyages IV'.

Chapter 17: Ennoia and Ophis

On Hart's Victrola, see Reed. 'I saw the frontiers . . . sands
running . . .' and 'interminably . . . stopped playing', *The Bridge*.
On the Ophites see the Apocryphal Gospels. Grace's annotated
Dickinson is held in Crane's Columbia archive. I quote 'If I
could see you in a year . . .' from poem 511 and 'This world is
not conclusion . . .', from 373. 'Be gone! . . . bedight' and
dialogue between Grace and Frances are quotations from the
seance transcript. 'The imagination spans beyond despair', 'For
the Marriage of Faustus and Helen'. Loveman's final days and
last poem are recorded in letters (Galpin Papers); Sam recalls
Grace's death in his Unterecker interview. The line 'inviolate
curve, forsake our eyes' is from *The Bridge*.

Select Bibliography

Alcántara, Isabel, and Sandra Egnolff, *Frida Kahlo and Diego Rivera* (Munich: Presetl, 2011).

Berlant, Lauren, 'Intimacy: A Special Issue', *Critical Inquiry*, 24.2 (1998), pp. 281–8.

Best-Maugard, Adolfo, *A Method for Creative Design* (New York: A. A. Knopf, 1937).

Boland, Eavan, *New Collected Poems* (Manchester: Carcanet, 2012).

Brenner, Anita, *Idols Behind Altars* (New York: Payson & Clarke, 1929).

Brodsky, Joseph, *Less Than One: Selected Essays* (London: Penguin, 2011).

Brooks, Charles S., *Hints to Pilgrims* (New Haven, CT: Yale University Press, 1921).

Brown, Susan Jenkins, *Robber Rocks: Memories of Hart Crane* (Middletown: Wesleyan University Press, 1969).

Brum, Blanca Luz, *Un document humano* (Montevideo: Impresora Uruguaya, 1933).

Chase, Stuart, *Mexico* (New York: The Macmillan Company, 1946).

Select Bibliography

Corn, Alfred, *Stake: Selected Poems, 1972–1992* (Washington, DC: Counterpoint, 1999).

Corns, Thomas, *Milton's Language* (Oxford: Basil Blackwell, 1990).

'Couple shot dead in artists' hotel', *New York Times*, 11 December 1929, pp. 1, 18.

Cowley, Malcolm, *Exile's Return: A Literary Odyssey of the 1920s* (London: Penguin, 1994).

—— *A Second Flowering* (Andre Deutsch: London, 1973).

Crane, Hart, *Complete Poems*, ed. Marc Simon (New York: Liveright, 2001).

—— *Letters of Hart Crane and his Family*, ed. Thomas S. W. Lewis (New York: Columbia, 1974)

—— 'Note on the Paintings of David Siqueiros', *La Exposición Siqueiros* (Mexico City: Casino Español, 1931).

—— *O My Land, My Friends: The Selected Letters of Hart Crane*, ed. Langdon Hammer and Brom Weber (New York: Four Walls Eight Windows, 1997).

—— 'Sr. Hart Crane, distinguido literato norteamericano, que se encuentra en Mexico en viaje de estudio', interview, *El Universal*, 18 April 1931.

Delpar, Helen, *The Enormous Vogue of Things Mexican: Cultural Relations between the United States and Mexico, 1920–1935* (Tuscaloosa, AL: University of Alabama Press, 1992).

Dodge, Mabel Lujan, *Intimate Memories: The Autobiography* (Albuquerque, NM: University of New Mexico Press, 2014).

Donoghue, Denis, 'Suicide Was in the Script: The Life of John Berryman', *New York Times*, 24 October 1982, p. 9.

Eastman, Max, 'Poets Talking to Themselves', *Harper's Magazine*, 163.977 (October 1931), pp. 563–74.

Fisher, Clive, *Hart Crane: A Life* (New Haven, CT: Yale University Press, 2002).

Freud, Sigmund, *The Standard Edition of the Complete Psychological Works of Sigmund Freud*. 24 vols., ed. James Strachey (London: Hogarth, 1974).

Greene, Graham, *The End of the Affair* (London: Vintage, 2010).

Hamalian, Linda, *The Cramoisy Queen: A life of Caresse Crosby* (Carbonadale, IL: Southern Illinois University Press, 2005).

Hamann, Edmund T., *Moisés Sáenz: vigencia de su legado* (Escuela Normal Superior 'Profr. Moisés Sáenz Garza': Fondo Editorial de Nuevo León, Monterrey, Mexico, 2015).

Hammer, Langdon, *Janus-Faced Modernism* (Princeton, NJ: Princeton University Press, 1993).

Hartman, Saidiya, *Lose Your Mother* (New York: Farrar, Straus & Giroux, 2007).

Hill, Geoffrey, 'A Pharisee to Pharisees', *Collected Critical Writings*, ed. Kenneth Haynes (Oxford: Oxford University Press, 2009), pp. 316–27.

Hollinghurst, Alan, *The Swimming Pool Library* (London: Vintage, 2015).

Horton, Philip, *Hart Crane: The Life of an American Poet* (New York: W. W. Norton, 1937).

In Search of Hart Crane: with friends of Hart Crane and his biographer John Unterecker, dir. Leo Hurwitz (New York: National Educational Television, 1966).

Irwin, John T., *Hart Crane's Poetry* (Baltimore, MD: Johns Hopkins, 2014).

Lacan, Jacques, *The Seminar of Jacques Lacan: Desire and its Interpretation*, trans. Bruce Fink (Cambridge: Polity, 2019).

Latson, Jennifer, 'Why Some Blamed Poetry for Sylvia Plath's Death', *Time*, 11 February 2015.

Logan, William, 'On Reviewing Hart Crane', *Poetry*, 193.1 (2008), pp. 53–9.

Lopez, Enrique Hank, *Conversations with Katherine Anne Porter* (Boston, MA: Little, Brown, and Company, 1981).

Lorde, Audre, *Your Silence Will Not Protect You* (London: Silver Press, 2017).

Loveman, Sam, *Hart Crane: A Conversation* (New York: Interim Books, 1964).

Machado, Carmen Maria, *In the Dream House* (London: Serpent's Tail, 2020).

Martin, Harry F. and Cormac O'Malley, *Ernie O'Malley: A Life* (Newbridge: Merrion Press, 2021).

Mariani, Paul, *The Broken Tower: A Life of Hart Crane* (New York: Norton, 2000).

Matovina, Timothy, *Theories of Guadalupe* (Oxford: Oxford University Press, 2019).

McLane, Maureen N., *My Poets* (New York: Farrar, Straus & Giroux, 2012).

Mircir, Melanie, *The Passion Projects* (Princeton, NJ: Princeton University Press, 2019).

Moore, Marianne, 'The Art of Poetry No. 4', interview by Donald Hall, *The Paris Review*, 26 (summer–fall 1961), pp. 41–66.

—— *New Collected Poems*, ed. Heather Cass White (London: Faber & Faber, 2017).

Morrill, Penny C., *William Spratling and the Mexican Silver Renaissance* (New York: Harry N. Abrams, 2002).

Munro, Niall, *Hart Crane's Queer Modernist Aesthetic* (Basingstoke: Palgrave, 2015).

Myles, Eileen, 'hart!', *Harp and Altar*, 6 (spring 2009).

Neagle, Michael, *America's Forgotten Colony* (Cambridge: Cambridge University Press, 2016).

O'Malley, Ernie, *Broken Landscapes*, ed. Cormac O'Malley and Nicholas Allen (Dublin: Lilliput Press, 2011).

—— *The Men Will Talk to Me: Ernie O'Malley's Interviews with the Northern Divisions*, ed. Síobhra Aiken et al. (Newbridge: Merrion Press 2018).

—— *On Another Man's Wound* (Dublin: Anvil, 2002).

—— *The Singing Flame* (Cork: Mercier Press, 2012).

—— 'Traditions of Mexican Art', *The Listener*, 23 January 1947, pp. 146–7.

—— 'Zuni Rocks', *Poetry*, 47.6 (March 1936), pp. 304–5.

Ong, Walter J., *Orality and Literacy* (London: Routledge, 2012).

Patten, Eve, *Ireland, Revolution and the English Modernist Imagination* (Oxford: Oxford University Press, 2022).

Paz, Octavio, 'Nobel Lecture', Stockholm, 8 December 1990.

—— *Versiones y diversiones*, Mexico, 1973.

Porter, Katherine Anne, *Uncollected Early Prose* (Austin, TX: University of Texas Press, 1993).

Reed, Brian, *Hart Crane: After his Lights* (Tuscaloosa, AL: University of Alabama Press, 2006).

Rivera Garza, Cristina, *La Castañeda Insane Asylum: Narratives of Pain in Modern Mexico* (Norman, OK: University of Oklahoma Press, 2020).

Scott, John W., *Natalie Scott: A Magnificent Life* (Gretna: Pelican, 2008).

Sedgwick, Eve Kosofsky, *Tendencies* (Durham, NC: Duke University Press, 1993).

Siqueiros, David Alfaro, *13 Grabados* (Taxco: 1930).

Stein, Philip, *Siqueiros: His Life and Works* (New York: International Publishers, 1994).

Symons, Julian, 'Hart Crane', *Poetry*, 54.5 (1942), p. 248.

Tate, Allen, 'Hart Crane and the American Mind', *Poetry*, 40.4 (1932), pp. 210–16.

—— 'In Memoriam Hart Crane', *Hound & Horn*, 5 (July–September 1932), pp. 612–19.

—— 'A Poet, and his Life', *Poetry*, 50.4 (1937), pp. 219–24.

—— 'The Poet as Hero', *The New Republic*, 127 (16 November 1952), p. 25.

Tavarez, David, *The Invisible War: Indigenous Devotions, Discipline and Dissent in Colonial Mexico* (Stanford, CA: Stanford University Press, 2020).

Uhlig, Robert, 'How poets' words can foreshadow their suicides: John Berryman, Hart Crane and Sergei Esenin', *Daily Telegraph*, 27 July 2001.

Unrue, Darlene, ed., *Katherine Anne Porter Remembered* (Tuscaloosa, AL: University of Alabama Press, 2010).

Unterecker, John, *Voyager: A Life of Hart Crane* (New York: Farrar, Straus and Giroux, 1969).

Vargas-Betancourt, Margarita, 'Continuity and Transformation in Central Mexico: "The Legend of Tepozteco" and the People of Tepoztlán', *Archeological Papers of the American Anthropological Association*, 25.1 (2015), online edition.

Walsh, Thomas, *Katherine Anne Porter and Mexico* (Austin, TX: University of Texas Press, 2014).

Wang, Esme Weijun, *The Collected Schizophrenias* (London: Penguin, 2019).

'Where Yellow Press Inspired Fear', *Daily Ardmoreite*, 14 June 1931, p. 10.

Williams, Tennessee, *Now the Cats with Jewelled Claws*, ed. Thomas Keith (New York: New Directions, 2016).

Wojahn, David, 'Tortured Visionary: A Life of Hart Crane', *Chicago Tribune*, 11 April 1999.

Yingling, Thomas E., *Hart Crane and the Homosexual Text* (Chicago, IL: University of Chicago Press, 1990).

Young, Ella, *At the Gates of Dawn*, ed. John Matthews and Denise Sallee (Cheltenham: Skylight Press, 2011).

Zinsser, Hans, *As I Remember Him* (Boston, MA: Little, Brown, and company 1940).

—— *Rats, Lice and History* (New York: Bantam, 1965).

Archives Consulted

Grace Crane Collection of Automatic Writing Attributed to Hart Crane, Special Collections, Ohio State University.

Hart Crane Papers; Sam Loveman Papers; John Unterecker Papers; Alfred Maurice Galpin Papers, Rare Book and Manuscript Library, Columbia University.

Hart Crane and Family Papers, Special Collections and Archives, Kent State University.

Ernie O'Malley Papers, Archives of Irish America, Tamiment Library, Elmer Holmes Bobst Library, New York University Libraries.

Ezra Pound Papers, American Literature Collection, Beinecke Rare Book and Manuscript Library, Yale University.

Katherine Anne Porter Papers, Special Collections, University of Maryland.

ORIGINALS

NEW WRITING FROM BRITAIN'S OLDEST PUBLISHER

2022

Catchlights | **Niamh Prior**

A 'clever, literary and intriguing' (*Irish Examiner*) novel in stories about shallow and deep acts of cruelty, love, selfishness and kindness which reverberate for years.

Nobody Gets Out Alive | **Leigh Newman**

An exhilarating, 'irresistible' (Jonathan Lee) story collection about women navigating the wilds of male-dominated Alaskan society.

Free to Go | **Esa Aldegheri**

One woman's around-the-world adventure, and an 'honest and perceptive' (Lois Pryce) exploration of borders, freedom and motherhood.

2021

Penny Baps | **Kevin Doherty**

A beautifully told debut about the relationship between brothers and the difference between good and bad by a 'new, original voice' (*Irish Times*).

A Length of Road | **Robert Hamberger**

A memoir about love and loss, fatherhood and masculinity, and John Clare, by a Polari Prize-shortlisted poet, 'whose work is rooted in people and relationships' (Jackie Wills).

We Could Not See the Stars | **Elizabeth Wong**
Han must leave his village and venture to a group of islands to discover the truth about his mother – 'There is really no book quite like it' (*A Naga of the Nusantara*).

2020
Toto Among the Murderers | **Sally J Morgan**
An 'exhilarating' (Susan Barker) debut novel set in 1970s Leeds and Sheffield when attacks on women punctuated the news.

Self-Portrait in Black and White | **Thomas Chatterton Williams**
An 'extraordinarily thought-provoking' (*Sunday Times*) interrogation of race and identity from one of America's most brilliant cultural critics.

2019
Asghar and Zahra | **Sameer Rahim**
A 'funny, wise and beautifully written' (Colm Tóibín, *New Statesman*) account of a doomed marriage.

Nobber | **Oisín Fagan**
A wildly inventive and audacious fourteenth-century Irish Plague novel that is 'vigorously, writhingly itself' (*Observer*, Books of the Year).

2018
A Kind of Freedom | **Margaret Wilkerson Sexton**
A fascinating exploration of the long-lasting and enduring divisive legacy of slavery by a writer of 'uncommon nerve and talent' (*New York Times*).

Jott | Sam Thompson
A 'complex, nuanced novel of extraordinary perception' (*Herald*) about friendship, madness and modernism.

Game Theory | Thomas Jones
A 'well observed and ruthlessly truthful' (*Daily Mail*) comedy about friendship, sex and parenting, and about the games people play.

2017
Elmet | Fiona Mozley
'A quiet explosion of a book, exquisite and unforgettable' (*The Economist*), about a family living on land that isn't theirs.

2016
Blind Water Pass | Anna Metcalfe
A debut collection of stories about communication and miscommunication, between characters and across cultures that 'demonstrates a grasp of storytelling beyond the expectations of any debut author' (*Observer*).

The Bed Moved | Rebecca Schiff
Frank and irreverent, these stories offer a singular view of growing up (or not) and finding love (or not) from 'a fresh voice well worth listening to' (*Atlantic*).

Marlow's Landing | Toby Vieira
An 'economical, accomplished and assured' (*The Times*) novel of diamonds, deceit and a trip up-river.